When winter comes—

...I had to reassure them that the loss .... was not just an accident or a whim of fate. Instead of asking the question, "Why us?" we looked at "Why not us?"

...God is especially close to those who weep and are broken hearted.... or the will to go on...

...It is a time ... for new directions in our lives... we begin to experience healing and to understand that grief is actually a gateway to new life.

WHEN WINTER COMES

USHA JESUDASAN

EastWest Books (Madras) Pvt. Ltd.
Chennai   Bangalore   Hyderabad

EastWest Books (Madras) Pvt. Ltd.,
62-A, Ormes Road, Kilpauk, Chennai(Madras) -600 010
3-5-1108, Narayanaguda, Hyderabad - 500 029
66, I Floor, 53/2 Bull Temple Road, Basavanagudi, Bangalore -560019.

Copyright ©2000
All rights reserved

ISBN : 81-86852-70-0

Price : 95/-

Printed at Sri Venkatesa Printing House
Chennai 600 026. Ph : 483 8543

Published by EastWest Books (Madras) Pvt. Ltd
62-A, Ormes Road, Kilpauk, Chennai - 600 010.

For

my beloved parents – Amala and late Dr V. Emmanuel

and

my wonderful brothers - Ramesh and Sunil

ACKNOWLEDGMENTS

My deep gratitude to:

My friends - Mary Ann Negi, Anne Dayanandan and Mini Krishnan who patiently read through my manuscript and gave many valuable suggestions.

My special thanks and love to :

Claire Emmanuel, my sister in- law, who tended to my wounds with gentleness and love.
Anna and Dr P. Zachariah, for keeping their hearts and home open to me at all times, for the caring and sharing.
Emma and Tharyan Koshi for enveloping me in their warmth and love.
Sara Battarcharji, who nourished my soul with poems and prayers.
Nalatham Manoharan, my best friend, for all her love and special care.
Renu Raju, often my companion on this journey.
Goutam Ghosh, my friend and critic, whose encouragement and faith in me helped me persevere especially at times when I felt like giving up.

My deepest appreciation to:

My publishers, East West Books{ Madras} Pvt. Ltd, for all their support and their willingness to share my journey with others.

My sincere appreciation and all my love to:

My sons - James and John, who graciously allowed me to share a very personal part of their lives.

Mallika, my darling daughter, for keeping me alive with her love and hugs and kisses.

USHA JESUDASAN

INTRODUCTION

Nothing in life's experiences prepares us for the loss of someone dear to us. Nothing prepares us for the depth and range of feelings that suddenly turn our lives up side down. Feelings that numb us. Feelings that make us crumple with pain. Feelings which suddenly overwhelm and threaten to drown us. Often there are no words to describe how we feel.

This book is a record of a journey through the most difficult period of my life when everything crashed around me - my identity, self esteem, my sense of belonging, my creativity. My faith too seemed to desert me. The pain paralyzed me, the future seemed bleak and hopeless. There were days when I wondered if I would ever function as a normal human being again.

To be able to live again we need to be able to face the pain, the anger and ask all the questions for which there may never be answers.

Most bereaved people put on a brave face, and struggle on, covering their pain. Our busy modern way of life and superficial relationships allow no room for experiencing grief as a long healing process. It is not easy to be with people who grieve or are in any kind of pain. Tears are embarrassing to those who are not in pain. And so the bereaved are often denied the companionship they badly need to articulate their feelings, to understand what has happened to them. The easiest thing to do is to retreat into a shell and keep these feelings to oneself. To die a little slowly inside everyday, while remaining 'normal' on the outside.

It was a very lonely time. There was no one who could share my pain, who could understand my confused thoughts and fragmented feelings. Whenever I raised them it made those close to me uncomfortable. So being a writer, the agony, the fears, the feelings of loneliness and confusion took shape in my journals. My anguished thoughts and words enabled me to see that to begin again, I needed to understand and respect my feelings of despair, sadness and anger. These were legitimate and natural feelings to which I had a right. Once I understood them, I needed to come to a point of acceptance and peace. From feeling hopeless I had to cling to hope. From feeling helpless I had to come to a point where I was willing to take responsibility for myself. From loneliness I had to move on to solitude. From feeling abandoned to being loved again. I knew that all this would not be handed to me on a silver plate. I would have to discover it for myself.

So I began the journey. As the cold barren landscape of the winter of my life slowly receded, the surprises and joyfulness of spring came into view. I rediscovered myself. I found new strengths within me. New hope. New friends. New meaning for my life. I discovered that in any circumstances, when winter comes, spring is never far behind.

One does not have to lose a loved one to go on this kind of journey. It is a journey we all need to make at some point in our lives. I hope this book will speak to those who are moving from a the winter in their lives in search of spring.

USHA JESUDASAN
August 2000

CONTENTS

1.	Grief Is……	1
2.	The Mystery Of Pain And Suffering	9
3.	All May Be Lost – But Love Remains	15
4.	Hope And Comfort	20
5.	A Change In Identity	36
6.	Holding The Family Together	46
7.	Facing The Loneliness	53
8.	From The Desert Of Loneliness – To The Garden Of Solitude	66
9.	A New Life	71
10.	The Journey Continues	79

GRIEF IS ....

A fresh breeze brushed against my cheek as I sat on my chair on the verandah. The rising warmth of a new morning, the sounds from the kitchen, the clattering of the milkman's tins, the ringing of the telephone ..... just the normal beginning of another day. Glancing at my watch, I got up. It was time to give Kumar his medicines. As I stood up, something sharp tore into my heart, and I crumpled in pain. Then, the awful realization hit me. He was gone. There was no need for any more medicines. Death had slowly crept up and taken away my husband.

"Sit down," a voice inside me said. "The days of watching, worrying, pain and anguish, are over." What then was this terrible feeling inside me? Was it pain? No, it wasn't. Not exactly. It wasn't anything I had known before, so I could not give it a name. I felt numb. Someone placed a cup of steaming hot coffee in my hand. I raised it to my lips knowing that it was the right thing to do. Strange that the heat did not scald me. The faces around me were so familiar - my mother, my brother and yet, I felt as if they were strangers; as if I were seeing them for the first time.

Why was I so cold when everything around me was so comforting and caring? Something inside me began to freeze. It started with my hands and then fingers of iciness spread up to my face and all over me. It seemed as if a frozen ball had taken over where my heart once was. "This pain, this coldness, this numbness….this must be grief."

I had always thought that grief was just deep sadness. My stomach tightened and it felt like a thousand clamps were opening and shutting inside me. Painful cramps one moment, a feeling of relief the next. Just as I got used to and was thankful for the release, the pain would start all over again. I was afraid. Afraid of being alone. Afraid of what lay ahead. I remembered feeling this way before my first piano exam when I was a little girl. Not knowing what to expect. Wanting whatever was ahead of me to go away. No one ever told me that grief was so frightening.

The day stretched out like a yard of ribbon in front of me. Usually, at this time I would be seeing to Kumar's breakfast, checking the temperature of his bath water, sorting out his medicines. With that routine snatched away from me, I had no idea what to do with myself for the rest of the day. So much of our life flashed past me. Kumar slipping a ring on my finger for the first time. Kumar playing with the children, chopping wood in the garden, revving up his motorbike. The long walks together at sunset, the warm caresses and kisses. The moments of tenderness and softness after we had made love. None of this would ever be a part of my life again. I would never hear his laughter, or hear him bang on the door impatiently. Never feel the warmth of his body against mine. Never see a flash of his smile, or the gleam in his eyes. The tears which till now I had tried to hide, just flowed and flowed. The sense of loss and loneliness increased as I thought of time passing by without him. Grief must be this intense sadness, a sadness that breaks your heart into tiny pieces.

I wandered through our home like a stranger, picking up things and wondering, "Is this really mine?" It was bewildering. Of course this was my home. I had lived in it for the past seventeen years. Every single thing in this house was chosen by me, and placed in its particular place by me; yet, it no longer felt like my home. The glass and silver and all the beautiful things which we had collected and so loved seemed quite obscene now.

"Where did this come from?" I thought, as I held a little box made of shells. Then I remembered that it was something Kumar had bought me as an anniversary gift. Tiny 'couples' of shells formed one large heart. It lay in my hand, a sad reminder of a life lost to me now.

The numbness quickly lifted as another feeling spread through me. The coldness had gone, overtaken by a raging fire burning within me. How could this have happened to me? How could all that I knew and loved, end so quickly? Why did it all have to end so soon? The gleaming bits of mother of pearl stared up at me. Of what use was this to me now? I didn't want this box, I wanted the man who gave it to me. I never wanted to see it again. It crashed against the floor and shattered into pieces. Just the way my heart felt inside me. Broken into a thousand little fragments.

On hearing the noise, the children came in and sat down beside me on the floor, and held me. All of us were crying. They cried because they were shocked at seeing me destroy something so beautiful and precious, and had never seen me in such a state before. I wept, because I could not understand what was happening to me. I was frightened now by the anger and violence within me. No one ever told me that grief was violent and destructive. How could I have known that it would leave me feeling so mutilated, raw and wounded?

When the pain, fear and sadness hit me, I thought to myself, " This can't be happening to me. It must be some kind of a nightmare. Maybe if I don't think about it, it will go away." But of course it didn't. It remained an uninvited guest, assuring me that it was going to stay. Grief had shattered my feelings of belonging, of safety.

When we recalled things that Kumar did or said, we sometimes laughed. The sound of our laughter caused us enormous pain. We would look at each other, tears welling up. Could we laugh this way when we had just lost the person we loved most? When we had seen him suffer, waste away and finally die? It seemed indecent and made us feel guilty. Yet, our memories of him were happy ones, and remembering them made us happy for a few moments too. No one ever told me that grief was a time of confusion, of bewilderment, of a strange kind of guilt.

Grief and loss were strangers to us. They came into our lives uninvited. From that point onwards pain, sadness, anger, confusion, fear and loneliness would be our daily companions. We could not shoo them away, or politely show them the door. We could not ignore them, nor pretend that they did not exist. They had come to stay. We would have to learn how to live with them as so many others had done. There were times when we thought that we were unfairly singled out, that we were the only ones who had suffered loss. But it was not so.

One day, Savithri, a lady whom I did not know till then, and who was much younger than I was, came and sat beside me and shared her experience. "It was a Saturday morning," she said, "My husband went to see a friend and he left promising to return quickly. It seemed like he had been gone just a few moments when there was a ring at the door. There they stood, strangers I had never seen before, with the body of my husband. There was no blood, no obvious sign of injury, so I found it hard to believe he was dead. My mouth was so dry I could hardly speak. Someone wanted the phone number of my brother, and although I knew it by heart I could not recall it at that time. My mind had gone completely blank. I could not think of anything for a long while. My neighbours came in then and called my family. Grief was frightening, and painful, but with the support of family and friends, life slowly took on a different pattern. I took over the business, and made a new life for myself and the children. Today as you can see there is a measure of happiness in our lives." Her warm hands on mine were reassuring.

"Time heals," she said. Her gentle eyes, moist with unshed tears promised healing with time. As she left, she placed a beautiful card into my hands which said,

"There is no heartbreak that heaven cannot heal."

I knew that it was not always so, for Ranjini shared how her daughter had died when she was just six months old. "To other people she was just a baby, but to me she was my first child. I was heartbroken. The grief that I felt, trapped me into a shell of loneliness and anger. Life had been so unfair. I could not share my pain with anyone. It stayed within me. Later on I had other children, but something inside me died with that baby. It is almost twenty years now, but I have never been able to come to terms with it. The grief and pain of that loss still remains." Grief, it seemed could also be never ending.

Every death brings deep pain and grief, for it is a parting from a loved one. Death has the power to destroy, to tear apart, to devastate, to isolate. Grief has the same power too. As I groped around, looking for people to identify with, I came to realize that grief is not always due to bereavement. There is the grief too of the unacceptable and from an inescapable situation. The situation from which there is no relief, no way out, and often very little hope. The grief of a parent with a child who has special emotional and physical needs and requires constant attention and care; the grief of children who have to care for elderly parents who are so old and child—like again; the grief of those who have to live with mental illness in someone they love; the grief of someone who has a loved one in prison.

Every kind of grief brings with it feelings of emptiness and loneliness, neglect and alienation as well as intense pain and suffering. There were days when weeping silently, holding a pillow for comfort is all that is possible. The doors would be closed, the night quiet and still, my soul bared and torn into shreds. When my eyes were dry for a while, I would raise them up and ask,

" Why?"

"Why am I still weeping after all this time?

Why have I made no progress despite trying so hard? Why am I not able to experience the healing that time ought to bring?"

Such questions clawed at my soul often. There seemed to be no answers to such questions and the weeping, sadness and despair just increased. Not only did I have to cope with grief, but also with the guilt of not getting over the grief.

"Where is God when it hurts?" I asked, " Where is He when I need answers?" The silence is bewildering. I knew that I was not the only one to experience this terrible feeling of betrayal. C.S Lewis, writing after the death of his wife, in *A Grief Observed*, asks the same question.

Where is God when you need him? Go to Him when your need is desperate, when all other help is in vain, and what do you find? A door slammed in your face, and a sound of bolting and double bolting on the inside. After that silence.

The heaviness of suffering makes it impossible for us to understand how life can go on normally. The pain and suffering fills your whole being. It is overpowering and takes over every aspect of life. You cannot feel or think about anything else. It fills your entire horizon - you cannot see anything or focus on anything else.

When my eyes dry and my heart is a little calmer, I ask myself, " Is there any meaning in all this?" At the moment I am unable to see the big picture. I only see the shattered fragments of my life, and I wonder how they will all fit into any kind of pattern.

Many years ago I remember seeing the Chaldni plate. This is a brass plate fixed on a pedestal. A bow is drawn tautly across the edge of the plate and sand is randomly sprinkled on it. The sand falls in no particular pattern. If you gently touch the tautest part of the bow, the plate vibrates, and the sand is disturbed for a while. This vibration then causes the sand to fall into another pattern. Not one grain of sand stands alone, it all fits into a pattern. It may not be the pattern that the person who threw the sand expected, but nevertheless it is beautiful, ordered by the hand that touches the bow. My memory of this, and the explanation given to me at the time by the person who showed it to me reminded me that though the pattern of our life changes, there is an order into which it will beautifully fall at some point. I had to cling to this thought every time pain and sadness hit me.

THE MYSTERY OF PAIN AND SUFFERING

To someone facing pain, suffering and loss, it feels as if they have been specially singled out and broken to pieces. But as we look around, we see that actually brokenness is the norm. It is almost a way of life for many people. We see people caught up in tragic situations, difficult circumstances, accidents, divorce, death, poverty, disease and natural calamities through no fault of their own. The suffering seems undeserved, baffling and cruel. There is no justice to it. There seems to be no meaning in it. To those who are in pain, there is nothing that anyone can say to make the pain go away. There are no answers that make sense. It just has to be endured.

We see people broken and broken and broken again, trying to make some sense out of their shattered lives. Weeping, running away from their pain, questioning God, facing their pain, and finally learning to accept and respect suffering. Then we see their lives transformed and dignified by suffering. We see their lives deepened with special beauty and compassion, we see them set apart bringing hope and comfort to others in a way that they could never have done before their suffering. For pain and suffering is a mystery – a mystery which we cannot fathom, and therefore fear. A mystery which when once it touches us, surprises us and forces us to turn our lives around. A mystery which can often lead a person into the presence of God in an act of worship, submission and love.

Of course suffering does not always do this. Many people are devastated and worn out by suffering, and find it easy to neglect themselves, be self-abusive, and isolate themselves from all love and care. Often, unable to understand, or accept, it can also push us away from God in resentment, anger and bitterness.

Pain, suffering and grief, makes us feel crushed and shattered, closed up and cold. It makes us resentful of other people's happiness and their sincere concern for us.

" I find it so difficult to even talk to my children when they call," said Mrs M. " It is as if suddenly there is nothing to say. I don't want their advice, I don't want to know how much they care for me, I don't want to know how well they are doing. I just want to be left alone."

One of the worst effects of intense pain and grief is that in becoming so inward looking, we also become ugly and distorted inside. Not wanting to accept any help or comfort. It makes room for bitterness and hardness. It eats into us and makes us curl into ourselves, looking inward only at ourselves, unable to understand the isolation, the unfairness and the separation. Like an in- growing toenail,

The mystery of pain and suffering

it never stops growing nor hurting, but just twists and twists inside inflicting more pain than is necessary.

A mother who had lost her son in an accident shared how angry and bitter she was against God for letting this happen. " This should not have happened to him. He had everything going for him. I hate God now. I will never pray again. I have no time for God now, or for anything religious."

A young woman whose father suffered terribly during his last days, could not come to terms with all his agony and her loss. She had bottled up all her pain and grief and translated it into anger. " Why did it have to happen this way? Why couldn't he have died in peace? He was such a good man. I feel so angry all the time," she said. " I don't want to let go of my anger. It is the only thing that keeps me going."

The anger, bitterness and the feeling of unfairness are all a natural part of pain, suffering, grief and loss. The feelings of being completely out of control of one's life, of coming to terms with the fact that we have done nothing to justify this suffering, takes time to accept and get over. It is when we view our suffering as meaningless, without purpose that we go into deep despair and become hard and bitter.

To me at this point, the *Book of Job*, in *The Bible*, which epitomizes the depths of a human being's suffering provided a reasonable answer in my mind. Not that it explained suffering, or gave a blue print of ways to avoid pain, or even that it brought any kind of comfort. But it helped to voice my own pain. Job boldly says to God what most of us feel deep within us, but are too afraid to say aloud, lest we be punished more. He gives words to what is a tangle of confused emotions within us, he rages against the unfairness of it all. And each one of us who has been through any kind of suffering identify with him. In the end we learn that there are no answers, and that suffering is a large part of life. That it is through pain and suffering that we also reach out to God, and through Him, to others around us. And therein one can find the purpose of suffering.

Thus through this period of battling with pain and suffering, and coming to terms with the mystery of it all, my response to it changed from asking " Why?" "Why did it happen to me?" to, " How do I deal with it?" and " What can I learn from this experience?" and " Who else can benefit from it?"

Most of us will do anything to avoid pain and suffering. We shrink from it, we ignore it, we deny it. This I think is natural as we are not equipped to dealing with it in a manner that makes sense to us. But those who have been through much suffering and pain, described it to me as, " The gift that nobody wants." For only when we have experienced deep pain, do we also know what joy is.

Pain and suffering may seem pointless and futile, but it need not have the last word in our lives. It should not deprive us of the hope and comfort that life can still be meaningful; maybe life will not continue in the way that we had expected, but nevertheless our lives can still be meaningful in their own way. I read somewhere that Mencies, the Chinese sage, wrote that,

When heaven is about to confer something special on a man, it always exercises his mind and soul with suffering. It stimulates his mind, hardens his nature, and enables him to do acts otherwise not possible.

Though I had no great feeling for this sentiment, what he wrote next tugged at my heart and made sense to me.

Thus one who has not suffered cannot draw near to another in pain, cannot understand their suffering and cannot comfort another truly.

At this point, a friend who had lost her husband a few years earlier, took me by the hand and said, "At the moment it feels as if nothing will heal your pain and loss. Let me assure you that this feeling will slowly ease with time. Of course you must grieve and empty the tears and sadness from your heart. But there comes a time, when you have to accept the blow life has dealt you, and come to terms with loss and grief by focusing not on your losses, but on all your blessings, and all that you still have. If you resist and fight against the inevitable changes that must occur during this time, or if you turn bitter and resentful, your feelings can stunt you to the point where you will end up living in an emotional slaughterhouse. You will become a mere robot going through the routine of daily living. There comes a point when you have to take responsibility for your own life and reshape it according to your will."

I knew that what she said made sense. There was no way I could live the rest of my life with such intense sadness and pain. The idea of taking responsibility for my life was actually quite frightening. It meant moving from being a victim — to someone in control. It meant accepting the opportunities that would come my way, finding a cause to believe in and giving my life to it; it meant deliberately filling the lonely hours with things that brought joy, not sadness. It meant becoming a new person who looked at life through different eyes.

I needed to believe this and cling to the hope that the gloom that encircled me now would lift in time – that new hopes would arise from the ashes of despair – that new life could blossom from the greatest of disappointments. The card in my hand held words of promise that I would not have to do it alone.

True He wounds, but He also dresses the wound:
the same hand that hurts you, will also heal you.

ALL MAY BE LOST - BUT LOVE REMAINS

❋

One of the first things I learnt about our new life was that although death cut deeply into it and shattered the comfortable pattern and harmony that we were used to, life actually went on in the usual way. The day began and ended in much the same manner as before. Meals had to be cooked, children needed to be looked after, the telephone needed to be answered, shopping lists had to be made, clothes had to be washed, dried and ironed. All the mundane activities that made up daily life still continued in the same vein. And yet, nothing was the same as before. The sky was still as blue as it always had been, but it seemed a lifeless blue now. The postman still came with bundles of letters in his hands, but I no longer rushed to open them. Everyday just as the sun was going down, it beckoned me for my usual walk. Only I was reluctant to go. It made no sense for me to go alone.

There was a huge empty space in the place where another person once used to talk and laugh, share and please, and annoy and irritate. Kumar and I both liked a clean, well-kept home, and it had been my pleasure to keep it that way for both of us. Dusting, cleaning and tidying up were still necessary activities, but they seemed meaningless now and it no longer mattered to me how the house looked.

For the world outside, Kumar no longer existed in any concrete form. A painful duty that had to be done quickly was to clear up his room in his office. Several people offered to do this for me, but I felt that it was something I had to do myself. Our sons, James who was fourteen, and John who was ten, both offered to come and help me sort out Kumar's papers and possessions. Although it was painful for them the boys wanted to be a part of all this. Up till now, we had just held each other and cried. It had been too painful to actually talk about Kumar. Now for the first time we began to talk about him, and it seemed so natural as we picked things up, discarded some and put others away for safe keeping. Talking about him, looking at his things, and touching what was dear to him brought him closer to us and showed us some facets of his life and personality that we had either not known or taken for granted.

It was almost as if he was there with us, saying, "Here, look at this, do you remember this?" John's drawing preserved in his diary, a picture of Mallika and himself, a list of New Year resolutions Jamie had written when he was eight, and bundles and bundles of letters and notes I had written to him over the years. Seeing these long forgotten mementos brought us closer to each other in our grieving, and gave us an opportunity to talk about other issues that were on the children's minds.

The boys wondered about life after death. Is this life all that we have? What happens to us after we die? Is

All may be lost - but love remains

there really such a thing as a soul? Can Appa see us? Can he feel anything? Does he know what we are doing? Is he safe and free from pain? Is he really at peace like he wanted to be?

These were questions that had been floating around in my mind too. I had no answers for myself, but I tried to be as reassuring as I could be to them. This world may be the end of life as we know it, but I was sure that there was another life and world which we could not know of or understand from this side. As a Christian, I believed in the resurrection of Jesus three days after his death, and in the promise of the life of the soul being eternal. I believed too in a time when we would be reunited with our loved ones, when pain, suffering and grief caused by various tragic circumstances would be no more.

Later that night, as I sat alone, I was overwhelmed by sadness. Everything had come crashing down so quickly, including my faith. Much of what Kumar held to be precious, the various scientific papers he had written, the many awards and certificates he had received were all packed away in a large cardboard box. The memorial service held earlier had reduced a warm and loving man to just words and memories from a handful of people.

My mind started to play tricks on me and suddenly it seemed as if he had never existed at all. I wondered if this was all there was at the end of our lives – a feeling of nothingness, hopelessness and despair. I thought of all the pain Kumar had faced during his illness, the many times he went in and out of hospital, and how in the end, his acceptance of his disease and his early death brought him the peace he so badly needed to be able to face the end with dignity. Up till now, I had cried for myself. For my loss. And my pain. Now for the first time after his death, I wept for him. For his pain and his loss. And for all the sadness he must have felt at leaving us, and all that he had worked so hard for professionally for so many years. There seemed a futility to life that I had not noticed before. The finality of death and separation made me wonder if love and faith and all the things we had so passionately shared and cared about together were just figments of my imagination.

I was very distraught by all these thoughts and must have cried for a long time. Suddenly a kind of slow, gentle peace settled warmly inside me, and I heard a clear voice in my heart. "Don't cry for me Ushamma, I'm at peace now." It was trange as this was not Kumar's voice, but they were certainly his words. No one else called me 'Ushamma.' I didn't hear the voice audibly, but deep in my heart. I knew without a doubt then that wherever his soul was, he was still alive in the way that I knew him. He was not lost forever.

I couldn't understand why it was only his words that I heard and not his voice, but it was enough for me to know that he was still alive in spirit.

During our years together his understanding, love and ways of comforting me always made me feel special and safe even though many times the situations themselves didn't change. Now though death had severed us physically, here he was, still doing the same thing – comforting me. Death had not completely separated us. It had not destroyed all the love and warmth we had known together. It gave me great hope and comfort to know that life continues in a medium that we don't understand, that maybe it continues in a more beautiful way than we can ever imagine. Just as a caterpillar on a leaf cannot imagine what is in store for it once it spins a cocoon around itself.

It brought immense joy to know that love endures, even when the loved one is gone. I reached out for a card that a thoughtful friend had sent me and read the words which reemphasized the experience I had just had.

And if I go
While you're still here
Know that I live on
Vibrating to a different measure,
Behind a thin veil you cannot see through.
You will not see me,
So you must have faith.
I wait for the time when
We can soar together again
Both aware of each other.
Until then
Live your life to its fullest.
And when you need me
Just whisper my name in your heart.
I will be there.

HOPE AND COMFORT

❧

My faith in a caring God had upheld me during the days of Kumar's illness. Now I realized that my faith had to be stronger to allow me to trust in the same caring God, to guide me through the days ahead. Almost out of habit, as well as a desperate need, I picked up my *Bible* for reassurance. There were specific promises in scripture for widows, for those who had lost someone they loved, and for those going through all kinds of tragic situations which brought me comfort and hope.

Hope and comfort is what a grieving person needs most at this stage. Hope is the parent of faith - that indefinable something which helps us take a positive outlook in a situation of hopelessness. It often comes through other people and in the way they affirm us, through events, and in the remembrance of past experiences. We long for hope—that there will still be some meaning in life despite the feeling of hopelessness. Hope - that the sadness will eventually subside. Hope —that out of the grief and pain, joy too will emerge one day. Hope - that friends and family would still be caring and supportive. Hope too that one wouldn't always feel so despairing, so alone and numb.

Hope for me came from God, *The Bible*, and the caring support of my family and friends. One particular passage spoke more than others to me as it kept coming to my mind and to my eyes in cards and letters from friends.

When you pass through the waters,
I will be with you;
And when you pass through the rivers,
they will not sweep over you.
When you walk through the fire,
you will not be burned;
For I am the Lord your God.

I read passages where God had provided the facilities for a new life for those who were widowed, who had lost children and close friends, and these passages brought comfort and strength to me. At this point, the scriptures were the balm that soothed my wounded heart. I read the ancient Hebrew psalms used by generations of those who grieved and were in pain, and of those who faced traumatic or hopeless situations.

Much comfort came from poems written by those who had been through similar situations. One sent by a friend spoke directly to me.

Accept these tears as my prayer,
Watch with me please and give me strength.
I have no words to tell you what I feel,
You need no words to hear my cry.
Be with me please, and hold my hand,
For I feel frightened and alone.......
Throw your arms around me and comfort me,
See my tears, hear my cry,
Turn my pain into hope,
My loneliness into wisdom,
My fear into new strength for the new day.

I knew that I was not the only one suffering, that others had walked the same road before me, had asked the same questions, and had in time found peace and healing, even though the circumstances of their lives had not changed. This brought enormous hope and comfort.

Comfort also came when I chose to believe in positive truths, like the power of love and friendship rather than in my negative feelings which said, 'It's all over, nothing will be the same again. There's no one to care.' I knew deep within me that God did not want me to live a life that was empty and lonely. Or a life filled with pain. I knew too that there were many people who really cared for me and the children, so I had to harness these truths whenever I felt really low.

Much special comfort came from my brothers in the U.K. who stepped into our lives and took care of all our financial needs. When we found a house to move into, my younger brother Sunil and his wife Claire, accompanied me to see that it was the right place for us. "The last thing you need to worry about is things like paying your rent, so let me take care of it for you," he said. My other brother Ramesh put a large sum into my account so that I did not have to feel dependent on anyone, and said, "Use it for whatever you want. When it runs out I'll send yu some more." Although they were so far away, my brothers called every week wanting to know about all the little details of our lives. They encouraged me to be independent. They applauded enthusiastically everytime I overcame an obstacle or did something on my own for the first time. They sent us little gifts to show that they cared for us. During the first holiday season without Kumar, they insisted that we take a break at the seaside as we used to do before and sent us a cheque to cover all the expenses. " It just won't be the same," I cried. " We know that, but you need to do this. You need to overcome your fear that you will not have good times again, or be happy again. Although it will be hard, take the first step and you will find that there are still many things which you enjoy together."

Their wisdom and constant encouragement helped us move into new areas of life. Not great letter writers themselves, they frequently sent special cards with funny or happy caring messages for the boys and Mallika. They encouraged the boys by laughing and joking with them, and speaking to them of all the things Kumar had taught them and given them over the years. They reminded them too of the good times we all used to have together and assured them that such times would still happen. They had been very close to Kumar too, and by sharing their own pain and tears with us, they enveloped us in the warmth of their love. Their concern and the many ways in which they cared for us gave us a strong sense of belonging and made us feel secure and loved. This brought great comfort and enriched our lives in a very special way.

Much comfort came from my father's tears as he held me, reassuring me of his love and support and encouraging me in all the new things I had to do. This meant a lot to me, for I had previously seen my father as a stern man who did not readily show or share his feelings. A new relationship blossomed between us despite our pain and sadness. It enabled us to reach out towards each other for physical comfort. So often my father would keep me near him and stroke my hair or my forehead and bring to me a feeling of being specially cared for. For the first time we were able to speak to each other of many things in our lives and were able to understand each other both as father and daughter, and as two human beings.

Remembering past joys and sadness together brought a special kind of comfort. It also enabled my father to become more demonstratively affectionate and loving not just towards me, but towards the rest of the family too. There were more hugs and kisses. The relationship between us was transformed into something entirely different from what it used to be, bringing a measure of healing for both of us.

Thus in comforting me, my father too was comforted. It taught me that when death intrudes into a family, it isn't just one person who grieves and who needs comfort, but all those within the circle of the deceased person's life. It is everyone's responsibility to bring hope and comfort to each other.

Hope and comfort

My mother too was a special source of comfort in the way that only a mother can be. There was nothing that I could not discuss with her, and though she would frequently break down with the grief of her own sense of loss, it was comforting to know that our grief was shared. The kind of comfort my mother gave me made me feel very strong. It was not the soft coddling type of comfort which made me look at my own wounds the whole time. She made me look to the future with hope and showed me examples of people who had made it on their own. She pointed out my assets and my strengths, providing many examples from my childhood days when I had been particularly strong. She nurtured my need to be independent. And took me on wonderful shopping expeditions when my mood was low.

I had not realized till now how comforting letters of condolence were. As they poured in, they made me realize that there were other people, who were grieved by our loss too, and who shared our pain. It was comforting to know that someone still remembered and cared enough to write and share memories that were precious and good. This sharing of memories and the positive act of writing to show that one cared brought much healing.

Comfort came too from the community of well wishers which had formed around us when Kumar was ill. We knew that people still remembered us in their prayers - they sent us encouraging little notes and cards. They often called or visited. Many of Kumar's classmates from medical college, who had formed a strong loving circle around us when he was dying, still remained close to us. They continued to take care of us, being there for us, being part of our family circle, inviting us to be part of theirs too. One particular classmate, whom I got to know only after Kumar died, would phone me every Monday night and enquire about the week's happenings, encouraging me, listening to me, just being there for me. There would be little surprises for the children and me through the post when we least expected it. She became for me an island of fun and wisdom, a person whom I could run to with my torments, discoveries and hopes at any time of day or night. Once when I was feeling really low, a large pink envelope was delivered to me, with these words,

> *If I could bear the burden*
> *of your sorrow,*
> *I would.*
> *If I could but for a minute*
> *Take away your pain*
> *And make it mine,*
> *I would.*
> *If I could tell you*
> *There's a reason for this,*
> *I would.*
> *I'd do anything*
> *to take away your hurt.*
> *But sometimes*
> *The road of life*
> *Takes unexplainable twists,*
> *Unfortunate turns*

And the whole world
Seems cold and heartless.
But I want
To leave you with
This thought –
I'm here
If you want to talk,
If you want to cry.
If you can find comfort
In sharing silence with me.
You are my friend,
I care.

There were others too who took the time and trouble to call or write, and remember our birthdays, affirming us that all was not lost, that love still remained.

Leaving the campus where we had lived for eighteen years was a traumatic experience. I had come here as a young bride, with many dreams and so much happiness and hope. Now I was leaving it alone, with my dreams shattered.

Although the children were with me, and were looking forward to their new home, the thought of leaving our old home and driving away from it alone, really frightened me. A thoughtful friend who knew how I would feel arrived early that morning to help us pack, held our hands as we said our final good-byes and then drove us to our new home. Two other friends provided us with breakfast, lunch and dinner everyday for a whole week while we sorted ourselves out in our new home.

Not just food, but also the water, plates and glasses so that I would not have to wash up. Another friend accompanied me to the bank and helped me sort out all the legal matters and helped me fill in all the forms.

Saro and Marcus Devanand were members of our church. I did not really know them, but they knew Kumar, and knew that we were now without him. One evening they invited me home to spend some time with them and to meet some friends of theirs. It was a happy evening and the mangoes on the table made me reminisce that Kumar had always bought a basket of mangoes for the children at the height of the mango season. The next afternoon, Marcus visited us carrying a huge basket of mangoes. " For the children," he said, with great warmth in his voice.

All these practical assurances of love and thoughtfulness when we felt afraid and unsure of ourselves brought much comfort and the hope that perhaps things won't be as bad as we feared it would be. We learnt that such love and care is the fabric of human existence. That it didn't just happen. That it was the result of someone else's thoughtfulness, care and love for us. In learning to receive graciously from my friends, I experienced the true fullness of love and concern that God intends us to have in our daily lives. Such continued support, care and love brought new meaning and depth to all our relationships and showed us that grief can transform both the person who is grieving and the one who brings comfort.

A young teenager saw me sitting alone in church one Sunday and came to speak to me after the service. "How are you really aunty?" she said. " I used to see you and Dr Kumar together and it's so sad to see you alone now." I recognized her, but did not know her, and at the time was uncomfortable about speaking to someone so young about how I felt. Despite the very wide age gap she persistently reached out to me, often not knowing what to say. She visited me often, brought me things to read and sent me funny cards and notes. Within a few months we became firm friends and for both of us this was a new experience, a growing period – of learning to trust, of understanding someone completely different, and of learning to enjoy someone just for the delight of it.

Receiving so much sheer fun and silly laughter from her was hard for me at first. I felt that I had nothing to give her in return for all that she gave me. But as days went by, it dawned on me that it was important to receive all her love so freely given. It enriched my life enormously, helped in the healing process, and made us both aware of the special gift she had of being a care giver. For my young friend, giving so graciously was an important part of her growing up too.

It was through this community of friends and well wishers that we experienced consolation. The word consolation means " to be with" {con} " the lonely one" { solus}. We learnt that beyond pain and anguish, there were human hands that held us, cared for us, comforted us and brought God's love to us with 'skin on.'

The best form of comfort however came from the physical nearness and warmth of another body. Our baby daughter Mallika would crawl into my arms and stay there snuggled against me for hours. Making me feel soft and warm and loved again. Melting the pain away. Healing me.

While my own need for comfort was so deep, I was aware too of how much the children needed comforting as well. They had not only lost their father, but a whole way of life that they had been used to, a life that included a lot of outdoor activities like hunting, fishing and trekking. They had lost the familiarity of the home they had grown up in, and all the conveniences they had been used to. Jamie, usually a very lively and happy child became tense and withdrawn, speaking only when spoken to. There was never a smile on his face, just a pained blank look. He shrank away whenever I tried to draw him into conversation or into my arms. It seemed that there was no way of reaching out to him.

One night we had a flaring row over something very trivial and he broke down and wept. The reason for the tears did not lie in the issue we had just argued about, but in the denial of grief suppressed deep within him. Usually, I cried, and the children held and comforted me. I was not aware that friends and family had told the boys they had to hold back their tears and be brave for my sake. For it was a sign of weakness for boys and men to cry. Every time I wept, they just clenched their jaws, and remained silent, just holding me, and drying my tears. Now I felt their pain and anguish, and it hurt me deeply to think that I had ignored it all this while. I placed my own grief and pain aside and allowed them to find strength and solace in my arms and in our tears.

Weeping and tears are a natural part of the grieving and healing process, and yet it is so rarely allowed. We are expected to be brave and composed, to disguise our feelings, and keep them locked up safely. Mainly because they are upsetting to other people. And yet, tears are a physical, tangible sign of grief. I did not want it suppressed for any of us.

For the first time I realized how frightening life must be for them too. The boys knew that I did not have a salaried job. They could see that I was shattered and had little confidence in myself. They knew how dependent I had been on Kumar. They just could not imagine how we were going to piece our shattered lives together. They too needed comfort and hope and reassurances for the future. While comfort for me came from friends, my faith and other sources, comfort for them could only come through me, their mother.

At this point I had to garner every little act of kindness and care shown to us and remind the children that in some way we were still special to God and other people. I had to reassure them that the loss of Kumar was not just an accident or a whim of fate. Instead of asking the question, 'Why us?' we looked at 'Why not us?' It occurred to me that of all the people we knew, we seemed to be the best equipped to deal not only with the suffering that was part of Kumar's illness, but also with his death. We had faith that was strong, we were close to a good hospital, the hospital where Kumar had studied and had many friends. We were privileged to have supportive caring doctors and friends, and an understanding of this life and the next, which was slowly revealed to us during Kumar's last days.

We spent much time looking back over the days of Kumar's illness and remembering the instances when God had provided for so many of our needs through friends and strangers, and how such love had got us through the worst period of our lives. Looking at our loss and grief this way enabled us to focus on all that was positive and on all that we still had, and helped to take the sting of the pain away for a while.

Often when friendship and love is offered to us, we take it for granted, or worse, we do not recognize it as such even. At this point, I learnt to appreciate all the people who came into our lives bringing hope and comfort. The correspondent of Jamie's new school, Mr Harigopalan, took Jamie under his wing and became a father figure to him, encouraging him to shake off the lethargy which came with grief by getting up early and joining him for early morning exercises and sports. This physical activity also improved his appetite, and slowly his concentration at school began to improve. Next he encouraged him to take his studies seriously and gave him responsibilities at school and instilled in him the desire to be the best in everything. He encouraged Jamie to join him whenever he went out. They made special plans together and shared a unique relationship. His caring presence gave Jamie the hope that all was not lost, that there were still good moments, that he could still enjoy ' man things.'

Hope at this stage was more important than happiness for the boys. Hope that they would still do well at school and follow their dreams. Hope that we would still have good times together as a family. Hope that we would always be there for each other. Thus in trying to comfort and strengthen them, I found myself being comforted and strengthened too.

During the early days of loss, kindness and companionship are plenty. But as days and months go by, grief and sadness become embarrassingly unwelcome

Hope and comfort

companions to those who are not grieving. Our very busy way of life leaves little room or time for pain or sorrow of any kind. Life has to return to normal as quickly as possible. Grief has to be pushed aside, so that our routine can continue. Our deepest pain has to be covered up with a brave smile. Our emotions are supposed to be tightly leashed within us.

It is a modern belief that the ministry of comforting and healing is no longer necessary and that we should 'get over the grief' within a few months. The ancient outward rituals which once allowed for expressions of grief, and the long period of mourning are now seen as old fashioned and unnecessary. It is considered morbid to visit graves with flowers and candles. And yet we found comfort and meaning in these little rituals that helped us to come to terms with the finality of death and helped us heal.

The children and I placed a string of fresh jasmine flowers around Kumar's picture everyday. We visited his grave as often as we could, placing a carpet of flowers there. At the graveside we prayed for strength and comfort for ourselves. We said special prayers for his soul.

Many of our family and friends thought that this was a sad thing to do, especially for the children. But in fact, it was a peaceful and comforting time for us. We looked forward to our visits to the grave. After placing flowers on Kumar's grave, the children would also place flowers on all the other graves and clean up the area surrounding some of the forgotten ones.

In the quietness and tranquility of the ground beside the chapel where Kumar's grave was, I came to terms with several difficult situations and found the strength to make many of the decisions I had to make. For Mallika especially, who did not have many memories of her father, this was the place where she was the happiest. She would bring her favourite toy, or sweet, or wear her newest dress and collect all the wild flowers for him and tell him all the things that were happening in her life. When it was time to leave, she would just say, "Bye Appa, see you next time," and happily skip away.

Grief was like a roller coaster - one minute I felt strong and able to cope both with my feelings and the day ahead, but the next minute I was down in the depths of despair. Just when I thought that the sadness was getting bearable, some memory, or phrase, or a belonging of Kumar's would dislodge the calmness within me. The anguish would rise again like a huge wave and knock me down. Sometimes there was no energy to pick myself up again.

Grief within me was constantly battling with self-pity. What was the point of picking myself up, if it was all going to happen again the next time something reminded me of him? At such desperate moments the only thing I could do was weep or pray, depending on my mood. The weeping brought a measure of momentary relief, the prayers for comfort and strength to get me through just one more hour brought peace and release from the struggle for a while.

It is written that God is especially close to those who weep and are broken hearted. To me it seemed so true. At such times when I prayed for strength or comfort, or the will to go on, God always provided it. Sometimes the answer to my prayers came from a friend to join them for dinner. Or an unexpected visit from someone who knew Kumar. Or a letter from a caring cousin. Or a call from a dear friend. Every dinner invitation, Every offer to go for a walk, every visitor brought comfort and hope and helped in the healing process.

Looking back, I cannot identify any one statement, or one person or event which was the sole basis of my hope. It seemed that nothing very special happened to give me the security and comfort that I needed, except the faith I grew up in. It was this faith which helped me get through Kumar's final days. Faith and the love which I continued to receive through various channels together gave me the hope I needed to be able to rebuild my life.

A CHANGE IN IDENTITY

❖

The hardest thing to accept after the loss of someone is all the changes that this loss brings. To be deprived of the love of a child, a spouse, a parent, a brother, sister or friend is one of the worst kinds of pain we have to endure. It pushes us into a life we did not ask for, a kind of life we do not want, a kind of life that constantly breaks our hearts.

Yamuna who lost both her sons in a motorbike accident said, " The first year was a year of getting used to being a 'non' mother. Suddenly there was no one to wake up in the morning. No shirts to iron, no one to nag or worry about. No last minute instructions. Worst of all, no one to call me 'Ma'. Twenty years of being a mother, and suddenly all the joys and frustrations of motherhood were gone in an instant …..the largest part of my life just wiped out. For a long time I used to think and act as if they were still around……go through the same morning routines, cook the same quantities of food, buy their favourite fruit in the hope that they would return. We were a very close family and there was always loud music, their friends and the noise of jokes and laughter. Now it became a silent home. Silent rooms. That was the biggest change. There were silent tears and a silent barrier between my husband and myself. We both grieved alone, not wishing to cause more pain to the other, so we found little to talk about. That was another big change…..the change in our relationship."

The death of a spouse plunges one into a well of confusion and uncertainty. Everything that seemed so solid and reliable suddenly disappears. Overnight one becomes a single parent with just one or no extra income. Often one loses not only a spouse, but also a familiar and comfortable life style and the home one has lived in for many years. The emotional security and protection that a spouse offers is also suddenly gone. And often close friends and family too drift away after a while.

For a woman who has lost her husband, the most frightening feeling is the loss of her identity. A few hours after Kumar died, I was introduced to one of his friends as 'Kumar's widow.' It struck me then that I was no longer a wife, but a widow. For almost two decades I had been a wife. I knew my role well, knew what was expected of me and performed this with enjoyment and ease. I had a special status within the family and the community. Everybody knew me as Kumar's wife and related to me as such. Suddenly my identity was lost. I was no longer a wife. All the perks, the comforts and conveniences that went with being a wife were snatched away. Now I was alone the way I saw myself was also shaken.

I didn't know how to react when someone addressed me as 'Mrs Jesudasan' – as I no longer felt like Mrs Jesudasan. And yet to be referred to as a 'widow' was hurtful.

To me the word 'widow' conjured up images of shadowy, lonely women who stood on the outside, watching with sad eyes as life passed them by. Women who were poor and wore threadbare clothes. Women shrouded in black or white, with no colour or joy in their lives. Women with no purpose to their lives, who were excluded from everything that is vital, alive and joyous. I was now a widow and fought hard within myself against being framed within this image.

Up to this point I had been a person who made decisions regarding the home and the family logically and with ease. Kumar and I used each other as a sounding board for the many decisions we had to make. Now alone, I became indecisive......there were so many decisions to make.....Should I move back and live with my parents or should I find a place locally where we had lived all our lives? One of the children wanted to change schools, so which school should I choose? Was it right to even allow him to change schools at this point? I kept putting off making decisions in the hope that if I did not think about them perhaps they would just go away. This only made the situation worse, as it made me feel that I was incompetent and not in control over myself or situations. The indecisiveness also took a toll on my self-confidence.

There had been a time when I knew exactly what I wanted and how things needed to be done. Now every little thing confused me. There were insurance forms to fill, tax forms to fill, things that needed to be changed from Kumar's name to mine, and it all had to be done in a legal manner. Usually Kumar looked after the administrative and financial side of family life. Now it

A change in identity

was my responsibility and it made me feel disorganized, weary and bad tempered.

I found it difficult to concentrate on anything for very long, and my memory too took a battering. One day when the children were away, and I had decided not to cook anything, a friend arrived. Around lunchtime seeing that she made no attempt to leave I asked her if she would like to stay for lunch. " Have you forgotten that you asked me over for lunch in the first place?" she said. Being so forgetful made me angry with myself for being careless and slipshod with my life, and this feeling too brought down my self confidence. I felt as if I had regressed to being a gawky school girl again, unsure of myself, always needing affirmation and someone's approval that I was doing the right thing.

Till now I didn't have to rely on anyone else's good will or strength. In fact many people relied on mine. Now I found myself needing other people and their skills, and having to reach out for help. My pride too had taken a battering, knowing that I wasn't as independent or resourceful as I thought I was.

Part of the confusion in identity occurred because many relationships had changed too. Friends who were part of our lives because of Kumar's profession, who often ate with us and stayed with us, no longer regarded me as a 'friend' now that he was gone. To some family members too, to whom we were a source of strength and joy, it seemed as if I no longer existed as just 'Usha'. The way I reacted to other people changed too— it seemed that I was extra sensitive to what anyone said or thought about me. This made me feel closed, unsure of myself and cold to anyone who came near me, in the fear that I might get hurt. A friend advised me saying, " A lot of these things happened to you before too, but then you had someone to lean on and protect you and so were able to take things in your stride and laugh it off. Now that you are isolated and alone, you feel more vulnerable, so every thoughtless remark becomes much more intense and personal." Thus creating a new identity meant finding a mechanism that would help me cope with all these changes too.

Identity is thought of as knowing who you are, where you're going and what you're going to do with your life. We find identity in our jobs, and in our relationships with others. For the first time not only was I not sure of who I was, but I had absolutely no idea where I was going, or what I was going to do with the rest of my life. While remaining married in my heart, I could no longer claim to be a wife, and yet I wasn't single. I was a mother and had a young family to look after. I was the family's sole provider, a role that was new to me. I alone was responsible for the family financially, emotionally and spiritually now. For years, our lives had revolved around my husband and his work. Most of the time I was a hostess, making sure that everyone who came into our home felt warm and comfortable and well-taken care of. Although I looked after the needs of the home and the family, I was more than just a housewife. I was a freelance journalist and radio broadcaster, but I wasn't a full time career woman either. So who and what was I?

Sometimes it felt as if my identity as a person depended on Kumar, as if without him, I had no personality of my own. This I knew was not true. We each had our own personalities and identities. I realized that it was our 'togetherness', the sharing, the caring and the unity between us that gave the strong identity as a couple. It was this intimate togetherness that was now broken, and the new identity that I needed to build would have to be without that feeling of togetherness.

Finding oneself and beginning again is both a crisis and a process. It is a crisis in that it is something that has been thrust on a person suddenly without any warning or desire. It is a process in that it has a beginning and takes time. The changes which occur, begin slowly on the inside first where it is least noticeable, and then work their way to the outside. The changes cannot be rushed. They have to take their own time.

Although I desperately wanted to be healed and to begin again, being healed was not a comfortable experience. For whenever there is a cut or a wound, one stage of the healing of tissues is pain. As the torn, broken places in my life began to be woven back together, there was much pain …….but the result of that pain was healing which enabled me to surrender the old and familiar to make way for the new and uncharted. This was not easy — it meant relinquishing some of my power, and a certain amount of independence. It also required a lot of courage and faith in myself to begin to look at and accept myself as an individual.

So after years of dressing to please someone else, I began wearing the colours and styles I liked and felt comfortable with. I rearranged my bedroom in a totally feminine way. I organized a new routine for myself in the mornings and nights that did not include anyone else and which still made me happy. It was like a kind of rebirth – I was still the same person, but different.

During the first few months, my mind would automatically freeze whenever I had to do something new by myself...... " No I can't do that." "I can't go alone." " I've never done that before." It seemed that my mind not only froze, but was also on the attack against me. Breaking the barrier of fear and walking into the unknown was one of the first obstacles I had to deal with. I asked myself, " What is it that I'm really afraid of?" and learnt to identify it, so that I could deal with it step by step. Doing something for the first time like dealing with the bank manager alone, reorganizing my finances, dealing with officialdom, slowly gave me the confidence that I could do things on my own. This gave me the inner strength to face the larger issues that needed to be tackled.

Beginning again is a period when all old securities based on past relationships and resources are shaken. It gave me the opportunity to stand back and look at my life as it really was – there were things I did, friends I had, and events I was involved in officially as Kumar's wife. I no longer needed to participate in these activities now, so I let go of these with a sense of relief. This also made it possible for me to evaluate what was still meaningful and dear to me from the old days – my relationship with several of his patients and staff – and hold on to them. It was a time too of taking stock of my personal assets, strengths and weaknesses, and re-evaluating my goals and plans for the next phase of life. It gave me the opportunity to ask myself what really mattered most to me, what I wanted out of life for myself and the children. It was a time for new visions – both for myself as a person, and as a parent.

A change in identity

No matter what our age, or circumstances, it is important to have positive goals for the future. An elderly lady with whom I shared some of my hopes for the future shocked me by saying, "You shouldn't expect so much out of life now. After all you have had many years of happy marriage. You are lucky to have the children. Live only for the sake of your children."

Yes, I was lucky to have my children and was determined to make a home that was happy for them. But I also knew that I had to do more with my life than just live for the sake of the children. I had no specific goals or desires, at this point. I did not know what I wanted to do with my life, or even how to earn a living that would meet all our expenses. Thus finding some kind of work which would bring meaning to my life became absolutely essential for my emotional well being.

Most of us at some point or other are called upon to decide what to do with our lives. Whether to continue as before, or to walk along new avenues, or to pursue a forgotten dream, or to sit back and take whatever life hands us, or to just give up. For me, the time to make this choice came with the loss of Kumar.

During this period a book that helped me find answers to some of my questions was Viktor Frankl's **Man's Search For Meaning**. Frankl records the sadness, grief and hopelessness of Jewish prisoners of war in German concentration camps. Almost every one there had suffered some kind of terrible loss. For many, life was meaningless without the ones they loved. Some yearned only for the happy past and lived in the present by clinging to precious memories. They could see no hope for the future or purpose to their lives. Such people soon gave up on life and died.

On the other hand, those who held on despite their loss and difficult circumstances, and those who saw some purpose in their lives and a future ahead of them, survived. Their message was for me too.

Life is difficult, I learnt. Life is unfair too at times. But life is also what we make out of the tragedies and disappointments in our lives. What was important was not what I had lost from life, or even what I expected out of it, but the choices life now offered me. Was I going to accept them and face them as a challenge?

To accept the opportunities, face the changes, and to be able to rebuild my life I needed to discover and sharpen certain new qualities like a sense of independence, initiative, drive and clarity in thought. I now needed to nurture and sharpen them so that I could not only fend for myself and provide for my children, but also relate to the outside world in a professional manner. The only way that I could learn these was to reach into myself, and allow God, experience, my family and close friends to guide me. Reaching into myself meant understanding my fears, my reasons for wanting something or not wanting it, learning to express my feelings and my thoughts more freely with God, my family and close friends. It also meant being open to new ideas and suggestions without having preconceived views.

Usually our lives are filled with noise and activity. There is little time for solitude or silence or reflection. In searching for a new identity I learnt that sorrow, bereavement, grief and pain, are all "still" places of life, when our soul longs for communion with God and withdraws from everything else. It is a special time when we are free to ask Him, " Why?"

A change in identity

" What is the purpose for all this?"
" What do you want from me?"
" What do I do next?"

It is a time when we have to face our pain and our helplessness and pray for our numerous needs to be met — for guidance—for strength—for healing. A time when we can ask for new directions in our lives.

It is not always easy being with God, especially when our questions are unanswered, and all we hear is His deafening silence. Yet, it is in the silence and stillness, in the presence of God, that we begin to discover who we really are. That no matter what the tragedy of our life is, we are still children of God. He holds us in the palm of His hand. We are still beloved to him. This is the identity that will give us the security, confidence and peace we search for. It will always remain with us, no matter how bereft and shaken we feel. Once we realize this we begin to experience healing and to understand that grief is actually a gateway to new life.

HOLDING THE FAMILY TOGETHER

When death tears a family apart, the loss and grief can so easily destroy a happy family. The feeling of being a family is gone, as sad reminders hit from every angle – the empty chair at the dining table, the sound of a familiar voice missing, the interruption of an established routine. It is so easy to become just four or five people living together in the same house, coming together just to eat and sleep under the same roof. Home suddenly becomes just a necessary shelter, for it seems that all warmth and love has gone.

I had seen this danger through the life of a friend. To support her family the mother had to work long hours after her husband died. There was very little time to spend with her children, and they grew up in the care of an able servant. Although they became financially strong, their emotional bonds were neglected and became strained. The strain in the family increased as the children grew older.

I saw too the opposite danger of becoming abnormally close and inward looking. In another family

Holding the family together

I knew, grief brought the daughters and the mother so close together in an unhealthy way that they shut out all other relationships. All offers of love and concern from other members of the family were refused. Later on, the girls chose to remain single, as they did not want to go through the pain of loss as their mother had done.

There were lessons to be learnt from both families. My greatest fear was of becoming so isolated and detached from the children, that I would lose their love, or becoming so close and inward looking that all our lives would become warped and twisted.

While Kumar had been sick, all my attention had been focused on him. Now I had to spend time with each of the children, nurturing them, allowing them also to heal and grow and find their own identities. I knew that the children more than ever needed a solid foundation based on love, attention and understanding now. Initially the impact of loss brought us together and made us feel much closer than ever before. But as the days went by, each of us found our own ways of coping with pain.

Pain is personal and is experienced individually. Jamie began to spend much of his time alone in his room. John became quiet, withdrawn and hardly ate anything. Mallika who was only sixteen months old had screaming tantrums. Often there were harsh words, misunderstandings and anger between us now. For a long while during the days of Kumar's illness we had been extremely thoughtful, gentle and kind to each other.

The sudden flare ups and tears were new and frightening for all of us. The old boundaries had shifted in that now I alone was the provider, the lone figure of authority, the only person who could give them the emotional security they badly needed. If this was hard for me to accept, it was harder still for the children. Increasingly I found that pain acted more as a wedge between us, as a hard barrier rather than as glue to bind us together. So it became a particularly difficult task to keep us all together in peace and harmony. I desperately looked for creative ways of dealing with this problem. I realized that the way to do this was to make our home a place of refuge and comfort for us all, a place of beauty and serenity – a warm, safe cocoon where we could heal in peace.

While Kumar was alive, one of our routines was the time of family prayer in the mornings. We would gather together on the steps outside our house which led into the garden. It was a time not only of giving our day to God, but also of beginning our day with a special kind of closeness with each other, with jokes and laughter despite the early morning rush. This activity had died with Kumar. Now I resurrected it as a way of keeping us together and as a reminder that though at times we didn't feel like a family, we still were one. Spending time together doing even the most mundane of activities like shopping, watering the garden, planning weekly menus, going for long walks and learning new things together helped cement our relationships. So did talking, sharing our memories, pain and our tears.

Birthdays and special occasions had always been a joyful part of our lives. We held on to these traditions making them as festive and celebratory as we could. Most of these activities took place within our home. I made it a point too of doing things outside the house as often as

Holding the family together

possible, where the atmosphere was different so that we were a little more relaxed and the burdens of the home stayed away from us. A picnic now and then, a few days at the seaside, a long drive, a meal out— all these activities helped us grow into a deeper closeness and a new understanding of each other.

I sometimes felt that the children were growing up with only my views, my ideas on everything and their whole outlook on life now came from me. I saw the need of bringing others into our family circle to broaden their outlook, to make up for the missing person, and to extend our family relationships. We were very blessed in having friends who were happy to come into our family to take care of many of our needs. They were always supportive to the children, giving the boys confidence and the assurance that they were not alone. Mallika who had memories of her father yearned for male company. One friend whom she was particularly fond of took the day off one day and took her out for the morning. They drove into town, just the two of them, saw dancing bears and monkeys, visited the ice cream shop, read and coloured pictures together. This was the most special thing that ever happened to her.

The pain of loss was inevitable, and I learnt that despite a tough exterior, Jamie crumpled at the sight of photographs of Kumar, yet, wanted the best of them to be put out so that Kumar was still there with us. John went to bed wearing one of Kumar's old shirts, cuddling into his old blanket. Mallika bit her nails right down to her fingers whenever she was upset. It became an added responsibility to teach the children to live through their pain, so that gradually it would lose its power over them.

Living through their pain meant allowing their hearts to be broken from time to time and respecting their tears, their fears and their moods, while at the same time giving them a positive approach to life and strength to look to the future with hope. Reminding them that the pain which at the moment seemed like a turbulent river inside them would one day turn quiet and peaceful.

We learnt to trust each other with our fears and our hopes and also humorously tolerate and indulge each other with even those silly things which brought us 'comfort'. Like sweets and chocolates for John, balloons for Mallika and very loud music for Jamie. We knew that certain things over which we cried about only time would heal us. There were other things which we cried over in sheer frustration - leaky taps, fuses that went off in the middle of the night, doors which refused to close. We had to learn to cope with these ourselves.

For a while I stretched myself doing all the things that Kumar used to do with the children, feeling that they should not be deprived of these experiences. In the process, I found myself getting more and more tired and sometimes resentful of all the demands made on me. Until one morning Jamie said, " Amma, you cannot be Appa for us. We don't need you to do all the things he used to do with us. You can't take his place. All you need to do now is just be yourself. Just be our Amma, love us and be there for us."

After a while as life resumed its rhythm, there were still days when I felt exhausted. I was not as energetic as before, and even simple tasks and keeping the house tidy seemed so tiring. I was often snappy and irritable with the children. The tiredness was difficult to understand, until I realized that grief is actually hard work. It drains a person of physical, emotional and spiritual stamina. I learnt to avoid unrealistic expectations for myself, so that I would have some strength to cope with the children. I learnt too the need to take care of myself and to spend time and attention on myself without feeling guilty.

Whenever I went through a difficult experience, I realized that the children must be going through the same thing too. I was able to understand and articulate my feelings and had opportunities to share them with others. But they could do neither and just bottled it all up inside them. Often they seemed quite happy playing with their friends, or watching television, but the exhaustion showed on them too. Their appetites were low, sleep uneasy and disturbed and concentration on school work almost nil.

Mealtimes were always difficult as it was then that we missed Kumar the most, and the time too that we felt most disloyal to him. " Is it okay to eat so well? Is it okay to enjoy ourselves like this?" the children would ask. There would be a sense of guilt that perhaps we should not be so happy without him. The children made me look for answers with which we could face life positively, without feeling guilty.

We all had fears and hopes for the future which we talked about often. Jamie feared being pressured by family and friends into being exactly like Kumar, and following in his footsteps into the world of leprosy. John on the other hand, was determined to carry out his promise to Kumar to be a doctor like him. I wanted to continue doing all the things that Kumar and I had planned to do many years ago. These times of discussion were very valuable to us as it taught us to share our deepest thoughts and feelings with each other, without embarrassment or fear.

   I began to look upon pain and grief as a gift - a gift that we didn't want - but were given anyway. A gift that brought us all together in a close and loving way

FACING THE LONELINESS

Months after Kumar's death, such intense feelings of despair would hit me at unexpected moments - when I heard a favourite song, or a whiff of aftershave on someone. At one such moment, unable to bear the pain, I asked myself, " What is it that causes my deepest pain?" in an attempt to logically deal with the feelings inside me.

My deepest pain was that of loneliness and the feeling of being abandoned, of being left behind alone. The fear of insecurity, the feeling of not belonging to anyone anymore. The loss of someone who loved me and whom I loved. The loss of having someone to share the little intimacies of life that we take for granted. A late night cup of coffee, talking to someone about the ordinary events of the day, or sharing family news.

Loneliness, a feeling of emptiness, or incompleteness is the common enemy of all humankind, but it is an especially nasty enemy of the bereaved. For people in any kind of grief, it encourages morbid, negative, destructive thoughts which leave a person worn out. This kind of loneliness is an emptiness that no friend could fill. The children couldn't even begin to understand it . No one however well meaning could enter into this space within me. It was reserved for me alone. I could't share this particular pain with anyone as eeryone around me belonged to someone else—they all had each other, whereas I was single.

The loneliness only accentuated the deep physical desires, - the need to be held, to be touched, to be caressed affectionately. The need to be appreciated and recognized as a woman. It was hard to face this loneliness. Every time I tried, I was confronted not only by my wounds, but also by my powerlessness to heal myself. In some ways it helped to know that,

"Being alive means being in a body - a body separated by other bodies. And being separated means being alone. This is true of every creature, and it is more true of man than any other creature...... He is not only alone; he also knows he is alone.......and this aloneness he cannot endure."

However, it did not really help in overcoming loneliness in daily life. There were times when I kept myself so busy that it seemed that at last I had beaten it. Or I would deliberately put it out of my mind with all the strength I was capable of, but sooner or later, the loss of all that I had valued most, the companionship and security, the feelings of togetherness and intimacy would call out to me hauntingly, and the feelings of emptiness and loneliness would return.

I learnt that when you run away from loneliness, sooner or later it would catch up with you. If you dwell on it, and wallow in self pity, the feelings only get stronger and more powerful and overwhelm you. So, the only way to handle loneliness is to face it, and to stop looking at it as an enemy, as something to destroy your life. I had to accept it as part of my life from now on, and had to learn to become familiar with it, and even to like it.

This attitude of course was new to me. Until now, whenever I felt lonely I would call my mother, or a friend, watch television, cook, tidy up or do something to occupy my time and my energy. As days went by, easing my loneliness this way brought no peace. When all the shelves were tidy, the ache still remained. When I hung up the phone after chatting for an hour, the ache was still there. When someone else's door closed behind me, the pain was there just waiting for me. There was no magic cure for it.

For a while, a tablet which gave sound sleep eased the loneliness of the nights and stilled the cravings within me. This too could not go on forever, for it left me so dopey during the day. In desperation I asked a friend who had lost her husband many years earlier, how to cope with it. "You have to learn to live with it. It is like a bad scar on your body, which will never go away. No matter how hard you try to get rid of it, it will always be there," was the reply.

Strangely enough it was at moments when I felt most alone, when I felt that God had indeed completely abandoned me, that I was also really sure of His presence. Really aware too of a strength not my own, a strength that came from above. Almost always, strength was given to me through another person.

On one such morning, as I sat on my chair in the verandah, dreading another day alone, a lady I didn't know, but who knew my husband visited me. " I came to tell you that I know what you are going through. My husband too died when I was your age. And like you, I too had great difficulty in adjusting to being alone and building a new life. Today I am the principal of a small school in town. I came here to ask you if you would come and spend some time with our children. Tell them a story, and spend the day with us. You have been wounded in many ways, and you wonder whether you will ever find meaning in life again. Whether you will ever be happy again. The more you open yourself to healing, the more quickly you will be healed."

It was an offer that was hard to refuse. The school was a small happy place for poor children, and they made me feel welcome with a beautiful bouquet from the school gardens which they had made themselves. They gathered around me easily and as I told them stories of magic and fantasy, the children opened their hearts out to me with their own interpretations and questions, which made me laugh a lot. The smaller children clamoured to sit beside me, and there were lots of little hands hugging me. The day that I spent at the school brought much happiness and nudged me towards the road to inner healing.

Such moments also gave me the courage to ask God to give me strength just to get through one more day. With strength, directions also came as to what to do next.

Comfort others as you have been comforted.
Reach out in love as you have been loved,
give as freely as you have received.

Facing the loneliness

At first these instructions seemed so harsh, for I needed comforting myself. "Whom could I possibly comfort at this stage? There is nothing within me to give to anyone else," I thought. A little while after I had said this to myself, a friend lost her husband in an accident. "You know what it feels like. You've walked in her shoes. So go to her. Comfort her as you have been comforted," were the instructions I received from above. So, I put aside my own sorrow and went to my friend.

Grieving persons often thinks that they are the only ones who have experienced pain and loss, and that makes them very selfish. Sitting beside my friend, holding her hand and watching her weep, feeling so broken, I realized that sadness, pain and loss are part of the fabric of every person's life. It surprised and saddened me to see just how many people there were who faced some kind of grief.

During this period too, I met a woman who had to live with a sorrow which could not be removed – a child with very special emotional and physical needs. We reached out towards each other, each shrouded in a very different kind of pain. I understood a little of the loneliness and despair in which she was trapped. The strength and comfort I had received from others enabled me to befriend her and be the shoulder on which she could cry. Just as others had reached out to me, it seemed that now I too had a responsibility to reach out to others in pain and loneliness. My reaching out to her helped us both……..for her, it opened a window into another world, fresh insights, a different viewpoint, someone to laugh with …..to me it brought a new friend, an understanding of a different kind of grief and much healing for myself.

I realized then that God doesn't give us the kind of comfort that coddles us and makes us feel good inside, and cocoons us safely only within ourselves. It is never the kind of comfort that is meant for us alone. It is to be shared.

In the midst of grief, most of us are unwilling to recognize that there are others who face the same or greater pain, and we are reluctant to share ourselves with anyone. But when we do reach out and touch someone else with our love, our sympathy and care, our own pain is redeemed and turned into a blessing both for ourselves and for the other person. The comfort and strength He gives us sets us free to be strong not just for ourselves, but for others also. He allows us to be creative in our own way, according to our own talents, so that we can face the challenges of the new life that we need to move on to.

One pathway out of the desert of loneliness for me entailed walking with others who had lost loved ones or grieved in some way. I found myself spending time with those who had lost loved ones years earlier as well. I met a young girl whose husband died in an accident just months after their wedding, who after a period of time went on to becoming a social worker. As we began spending time together recollecting memories and talking about the many struggles we faced, we were able to reach out to each other in sympathy, understanding and a sense of humour. Our evenings together brought hope, comfort and deep sense of being with someone who understood and cared.

The real cure for loneliness I learnt, is healing interaction with other people. Not finding someone to love us and comfort us, but finding someone to love and care for and in a real sharing of deeper needs. Healing a broken heart involves keeping your own heart open to others in need. Soon after Kumar died two young boys, Suresh and Selvaraj, joined our family as my foster sons. Suresh was the son of our gardener from Karigiri, whom we had sponsored through school. All through the days of Kumar's illness he had been beside us, taking care of the children, keeping them company while I was in hospital, encouraging and comforting them. He had one more year to finish school and he moved in with us. Selvaraj was the son of one of Kumar's patients who needed a home in town. We had a new life, and a new home, but there was so much sadness. The children who were used to vibrant male company were suddenly left with only me. There was a huge vacuum where Kumar had once been, and as hard as I tried, I could never fill their lives with the same kind of enthusiasm, delight and energy that he did.

The arrival of these two boys into our lives brought so much unexpected joy, laughter and liveliness into our home. Suddenly there were five children ranging from eighteen to a year and a half to look after, and there was no time to think about myself. As the children blended together, shared their skills, their jokes, and began to grow together as a family, I began to see some kind of pattern in the tapestry of my life. The hardness and coldness of grief began to disappear as we melted into one large family.

Although the children filled my life with work and love, there were still empty spaces in my heart. There were still times when being alone, tore me apart. We had always gone to church together all our married life. Now it pained me to go alone. In a state of self-pity, I stayed home the first few Sundays after Kumar died. But that only led to more despair so I decided to stoically bear what I must. One Sunday as I was sitting in church feeling sorry for myself, I happened to notice another woman on her own. I had seen her on a number of occasions before and knew that she was single.

"How does she cope,?" I wondered, and was silently thankful for my family. Slowly I discovered a 'community' of women who were alone, either because they had lost their husbands, or because they were single, or because their husbands were away, or because they were old, and their children lived in different places. Making the effort to get to know them, and understanding and sharing their loneliness became a meaningful part of my life. I discovered the quiet joy of being there for someone else, and unearthed an unexpected storehouse of wonderful new friends for myself and the children.

We can allow ourselves to be overwhelmed with loneliness and self-pity. But when we rise above it, and look towards someone to whom life has been more unfair, and fill a need in their lives, our own emptiness dissolves as we discover needs within us being met also. My father died two years after Kumar. For my mother, Amala Emmanuel, it was a period of much sadness as she had lost two people whom she was so close to and had been dependent on. She knew that she was going to be very lonely living on her own for the first time. Although fears and anxieties loomed threateningly over her, she decided to embrace her loneliness and live with it. One day an excited call from her woke me up very early. " I have just come from a nearby slum where I spent the morning with some of the elderly folk there. For the first time I saw old people really neglected, sick, without adequate food or medicines. There was no joy in any of their faces. Most of them just sat there waiting to die, and death did not want them either. I have found something I want to do, instead of just sitting at home and moping."

My mother found two people to help her and rented a small house where about fifteen elderly people could come and spend the morning having a bath, a meal, a nap and tea before they went home. Two doctor friends offered their services once a week to look after their medical problems. In giving of herself, her time, her resources and her compassion, much of my mother's loneliness was eased.

After the loss of his wife, Mr Selvam started a small shelter at the back of his house for street children. "During the last days of my wife's illness, I was the one who did the cooking and looked after the house. After she died, I did not want to go abroad and live with my children. What would I do there? I don't even speak good English. One day as I was sitting out here, a small boy came and asked me for some food. I was all alone and had not eaten that day and I was hungry. Actually I did not want to cook only for myself, so I asked the boy to come in. While I was cooking he shared his story with me. I was so shocked. He must have been seven or eight, an orphan, who lived on the streets and who worked for a grocery store packing rice and other spices. I asked him to come and eat with me every night, really as company for myself. Soon he began bringing a few others who also had nowhere to go and who did not have a night meal. We became a small family. Now there are about ten little boys who come almost every night, and I have no time to be lonely. I am busy planning the day's menu, shopping for vegetables in the morning and in the afternoon I cook. The boys bring me all their news and make me so happy with their jokes and laughter. They in return have a father figure in me, I advise them and sometimes scold them too. I am not lonely anymore, my life is so full."

Sharing our loneliness with someone else has its rewards. But one can't be with other needy people all the time. There comes a point when we have to embrace the loneliness by ourselves and be comfortable with it. We have to turn the loneliness into a quiet solitude. A friend from England sent me a cutting of an article by Henri Nouwen, a Dutch priest. In it, Nouwen referred to the loneliness of the heart—the kind that I was experiencing—as a desert. This idea I could identify with easily, as a desert is desolate, lonely and empty. And that is how I felt most of the time. A desert is a parched place, empty and devoid of life. That too was exactly how I felt. Nouwen said that loneliness was a desert through which we could stumble around and get lost, and finally die there, or that it could be a pathway that would eventually lead us to God.

He also gave a different picture of desert life. In fact it is in the desert, where life seems barren and impossible, that suddenly a fresh spring of sweet water appears. It is around this spring that many forms of life can be noticed that would not be found elsewhere. Clusters of unusual beautiful flowers, strange little animals and brightly coloured insects. The air around the spring is cooler, fresher and invigorating . The weary traveller is

Facing the loneliness

refreshed after a sojourn at this spring. This too is the desert and it was certainly more appealing than the barren ugly aspect of it. For the first time I realized that there were two ways of experiencing loneliness.

Could my life which now seemed like the desolate desert, become like a hidden part of the desert that is green and full of life? Could I ever honestly begin to enjoy or experience the peaceful solitude that Nouwen was talking about?

A kind friend took me to meet her aunt, an elderly lady whom age and ill health had slowed down. Aunt Sara had lived alone for a large part of her life, yet as I spoke to her, she didn't seem lonely or unfulfilled. To her being alone was not a negative thing. She had made it a creative, beautiful and fulfilling experience. A talented artist, she had taken up teaching and imparted her love of colour and crafts to children who had special needs. Her home had warmth and the beauty of the artistic creations of many of her children. In a specially set apart place on her verandah, was an old fashioned white cane chair surrounded by plants and flowering shrubs, and a table on which lay her journal and her devotional books. She shared how after the death of her husband and her son, she picked up the shattered pieces of her life, and turned her unbearable loneliness into something from which much beauty could flow. But first she had to search for God and soak herself in His presence, asking him to help her through this terrible period of her life. "I had to face my loneliness, not fight it. I had to learn to like being on my own and being friends with my own company. To help me do this I made this beautiful space for myself, where I could be happy and comfortable. Looking out into my garden, drenching myself in its beauty and colour brought me closer to God. Thus my loneliness which was once something negative and horrible, was transformed into solitude—which was something peaceful, creative, nurturing and nourishing. From that point I was able to share my love and my talents."

My visit to Aunt Sara was healing. As I left, she held me very close to her and said, " No season of loss lasts forever. There is a turning point in everyone's life. Light does return, maybe very slowly and dimly at first, but then as the days go by it gets stronger. There is great power in the ability to love again, to reach out through your loss to other people, to create new energy, to use your talents." What would it take to bring about this kind of change within me, I wondered.

Like Aunt Sara, I knew that I too had to face the loneliness and acknowledge its presence and power in my life. Once more Henri Nouwen came to my rescue.

The spiritual task is not to escape your loneliness, not to let yourself drown in it, but to find its source. This is not so easy to do, but when you can somehow identify the place from which these feelings emerge, they will lose some of their power over you. This identification is not an intellectual task; it is a task of the heart. With your heart you must search for that place without fear.

This is an important search because it leads you to discern something good about yourself. The pain of your loneliness may be rooted in your deepest vocation. You might find that your loneliness is linked to your call to live completely for God. Thus your loneliness may be revealed to you as the other side of your unique gift.

I knew I had to search my heart and truly believe with courage and faith that just as He had brought me to this place of pain and loneliness, that He would lead me out of it in time so that I would understand it and embrace it as something that could nourish me and not destroy me. It seemed that at times nothing could soothe my sore heart until I read a passage from Joan Hutson, who having gone through a similar experience, shared her insights and the strength and healing she had received.

Lonely heart, stop running, stop searching. Recognize the aloneness you feel, look at it truthfully, honestly, courageously and lovingly. Admit your hopelessness in alleviating it. Recognize your inability to escape it. Then, in hope, not despair, lift that lonely heart to Me. Sometimes I will fill it with friends; sometimes with Me; sometimes only with the full understanding that I know and understand. Sometimes with not even that assurance. Sometimes I will fill it with my absence.

Your inner being, may passionately crave the heart of a fellow human being to talk to, to understand, and I may not grant what you ask. But I will give you understanding of faith to believe that I'm aware of your loneliness, knowing that it is not time to dry your tears. Sometimes time must evaporate them. If a friend were to wipe them away too soon, you might not grow as I have planned for you. Let my awareness of what you suffer now in loneliness be your companion. Offer it to me.... I can use it to shape you."

Thus I began to learn to embrace the loneliness that had now become part of my life.

FROM THE DESERT OF LONELINESS..........
TO THE GARDEN OF SOLITUDE

The journey from the desert of loneliness to a garden of fruitful solitude begins with time alone with God— a hard discipline. At first the only feeling I had was one of being abandoned by God in whom I had trusted through all the dark difficult days of Kumar's illness. At that time my faith had been strong. I felt that I could go through any storm or upheaval and come out of it unscathed. I felt that God's power and strength would never leave me. Yet here I was bruised and broken, lonely and scared. It was hard to come to God with this feeling of betrayal. The only prayer that came to my rescue and made any sense to me at all was Jesus' own prayer to God as He hung on the cross, alone, in pain and betrayed.

My God, my God, why have you deserted me?

I could identify with this desperate cry of abandonment every time I came into God's presence. At first, time alone with God meant just crying out my pain and confusion and longing to Him. " Take away this terrible feeling of emptiness please. Bring meaning into my life again. Grant me companionship and your peace," was my constant prayer.

There were times when my mind would wander back into dark, heavy thoughts and I would find it so difficult to say even the simplest of prayers and wondered if God even heard or cared.

Often I found prayers in the scriptures of different faiths that said exactly what I wanted to say, and used them too. It felt good to be united across centuries, across cultures and other religions, and to know that my needs were exactly the same as those who had gone before me with the same petitions. It gave me hope knowing that men and women had travelled the same road and had been healed.

To some, prayer and spending time with God may seem to be a sign of weakness. A 'cop out' of real life, a way of escaping from the reality that surrounds us. Most of us are afraid of emptiness, of space and want to fill it up with all kinds of activities, worries and fears. For me, the evenings when the children were at play were the loneliest times. I would wander from room to room straightening out sheets and rearranging the furniture. One day, not being able to bear the loneliness, I went up to sit on the terrace, and cried out a psalm from the bottom of my soul.

O God, you are my God
I am seeking you – But you're the God in hiding.
It's difficult for me to find you

when my mind is so divided and my heart is shattered.
My flesh longs for the warmth of your touch.
I want to be able to cling close to you,
but you seem so distant. I can't feel you close.
I want your right hand to support me.
I need to feel that support.
Why can't I?
Please don't hide from me.

I had spent so much time looking at the bleak side of life, nursing my pain, afraid of looking into the future. Sitting there, watching the evening sun spread streaks of glowing colour in the sky, seeing the leaves above me swaying in myriad shades of green suddenly brought me very close to God. Listening to the high pitched sound of sparrows and breathing the fragrance of the flowers below made me aware of the beauty and peace that was still available to me. It gave me the opportunity for stillness and deep reflection.

As I sat quietly lost in thought, I felt that if only I could hold someone, if only someone would hold me, if I could feel gentleness again, or tenderness and warmth, then I would have some peace, some meaning in my life once more. Even as I thought this, deep down I knew that it could not be so.

I began to realize that the empty spaces within me could never be filled by any one person. In fact I slowly understood that there had always been a restlessness within me. The need for being 'whole' and not just a 'half' or a part of someone else had always been strong within me. When I really thought about it, although

Kumar had been my constant companion and we had shared so much together, there had been times in our lives when I felt an ache for something more.

Thou hast made us for Thyself
and our hearts are restless until they find their all in Thee,

said Saint Augustine hundreds of years ago. It seemed as if it were true for me.

Feeling the cool breeze against my face amidst so much beauty and quietness gave me the courage to come to terms with so much loss. I learnt to sit quietly on the terrace and enjoy the coolness, and not be afraid of being on my own. The peace of God ministered to me daily at these moments and I began to look forward to my times alone. Slowly I found myself extending the time I spent alone. Eyes shut, I learnt to empty my mind. The sense of calm began to be a part of me. A very happy part of me. A very necessary part of me.

For me these hours of solitude helped me to truly reach out for God with all my heart and soul. It took me away from everyday concerns, monotonous routines and deadly fears that threatened to suck my life out. I felt that I was in a place where I was able to rise above all this, even if only for a short time. It helped me to face the challenges that lay ahead of me with the sure knowledge that I was not alone.

The less I feared being alone, the more comfortable I became with solitude. I didn't need someone around me all the time. I didn't need the constant reassurances that I mattered, that I was beloved to someone, that I needed someone else's approval. I learnt to enjoy going out alone, sleeping alone, and being on my own. Appreciating solitude enabled me to journey to the centre of my heart. I found a new anchor for my life in my spiritual resources. I realized that previously my emotional life had depended on other people and on events which were sometimes beyond my control. But my spiritual life really depended on God, on prayer and on the strength and insight the scriptures and other inspiring reading gave me. Solitude made me reach out towards God and search for what I was to do with the next phase of my life. It sharpened the listening areas in my heart for God's voice.

So far I had been content to be a wife and then a mother. In converting the loneliness to solitude, and in allowing the times of solitude to be a time when I could listen to the voice of God in my heart, I was also able to discover my real vocation – my calling as a human being.

A NEW LIFE

A few days before Kumar died, he dictated an article that he wanted to give to his doctor Anand Zachariah. He felt that it might help Anand to understand the feelings and anxieties of other terminally ill people. It was a very moving article, and I typed it out and passed it on to Dr Zachariah after Kumar died. A few weeks later, a lady phoned me and said that her doctor had shared this article with her as her husband too was suffering from a terminal illness. Kumar's article had helped her to understand some of her husband's thoughts and frustrations. Over the weeks that followed, I found myself photocopying this article for many patients who were at the Christian Medical College Hospital at Vellore. Every time the reaction was the same. That of gratitude for sharing it. The Faith and Healing Cell at Vellore, which is associated with the Christian Medical Association of India asked me whether I would consider enlarging the article and retelling it as our story of facing death and dying in dignity.

I was not sure at that point that I had the strength or the desire to share something so personal and painful with anyone else. Till now I had been a freelance journalist, and a writer for children. I wasn't sure that I was equipped with the skills for such a daunting venture. I had no idea where to start and my heart was heavy with the responsibility of such a huge task. There were many doubts too. Death after all is the most unavoidable of all experiences. It is also the most common of human events. I wondered if anyone else would be interested in our story. Most people who fall ill find competent doctors, go into hospital, and either get better or wait for their disease to progress naturally and eventually die, leaving their families to pick up the pieces. We were no exception.

Kumar's story was also essentially the story of Christian faith. Would a person of another faith find meaning in it? Would any publisher find this story interesting enough to publish it? There were all kinds of doubts.

At the same time, I was also aware that for some reason as we went through this period of sickness, pain and death as a family, we were given special strength from above. People whom we had never known before entered our lives, took care of us, and brought meaning and joy into Kumar's life, enabling him to die in dignity and in peace. I was never able to understand why we were singled out for so much love and care from our family, friends and total strangers.

A while after Kumar died I heard about another family who had gone through a similar experience, but were unable to accept the terminal verdict of the disease. They were unable to share their feelings with each other and as a result each person within that family carried his or her own pain and fears silently, alone. The person who was dying too was locked in a lonely prison of his own. When the inevitable end came, their faith and hope of healing crashed and left them bitter, betrayed and empty.

Since then I have seen so many families go through the same situation of despair in utter loneliness. They faced so much pain on their own, missing out on what could easily be not just the saddest time of their lives, but also the best. I realized then, that the most personal is also the most universal, regardless of culture and faith. That pain, fear, doubt and tears belong to us all. Perhaps the story needed to be told, as it was not just about death and dying, but also about a caring supportive community which drew together in the face of tragedy. Still, I was unsure and hesitant about writing our story for everyone to read.

One day a young woman from Bangalore came to visit me, and told me how much Kumar's article had meant to her and her husband. " You have no idea what this article did for us," she said, holding out an almost tattered copy in her hand. " For the first time we really talked and talked and that made all the difference. We were able to accept his cancer not as a great tragedy that sought to separate us, but as something that really brought us together in the end. Both of us were at peace when he died. Thank you for sharing your experience with us."

Her visit left me shaken. There was no doubt in my mind now that this was what God wanted me to do at this point. I went on to write *I Will Lie Down In Peace*.

Now I marvel at the depth of loneliness, that desperate gnawing ache at the centre of my being that directed me to reach out to God and turn this painful feeling into solitude. The peaceful solitude I had been able to cultivate then enabled me to hear the call to write this story. By writing it innumerable blessings have been showered not only on me, but on others as well.

Having written the story, I sent off sample copies to several publishers. Mr Padmanabhan, from East West Books replied almost immediately. He further encouraged me by offering to donate the proceeds from this book to the work that Kumar had dedicated his life to — leprosy work. The children and I were delighted by his offer. Mr Padmanabhan said that he would ask one of his best editors to edit the book and he wondered if I knew her. The editor he suggested was Asha Nehemiah, a close friend of ours who lived only four doors away. Then came the difficulty of finding a suitable title. Time was running out. Somehow I knew that at the right time I would be given the right title. After all, the story itself was given to me, the publisher and right editor had been sent to me. Was I asking too much of God to provide me with the title too? Many friends were exasperated with me at this point.

Dr Zachariah, a friend who had closely read my manuscript and encouraged me to write the book felt that I should choose from one of the many quite suitable titles I already had in mind. The day before the deadline, he called me and said, " As I was falling asleep last night, a verse came to my mind. How about 'I will lay me down in peace?' I felt as if an electric current had gone through me. For just a few nights before when I couldn't sleep, as usual I had reached out for my Bible for something to read and came across Psalm Four. I had jotted down a verse in a modern paraphrase, which spoke deeply to me.

A new life

> "*I will lie down and sleep in peace,
> for you alone, O Lord make me dwell in safety.*"

I Will Lie Down In Peace. It was the perfect title.

Then we had to decide on a cover for the book. The children and I looked at every book we had in the house, and finally chose one that was simple and elegant. Mr Menon who was to design the cover was not too keen on what I had in mind and offered to come up with something different. When I saw the cover for the first time, I was amazed. It was exactly like the spot where Kumar is buried in Karigiri. The same spray of leaves from a thorn bush shades his grave, and the soft muted colours on the cover of the book are in fact the colours of twilight time in Karigiri. Mr Menon did not know this, neither had he read the book. He just went by the title. So it is a book that is not wholly my own, but has had the involvement of many people brought together by God in a strange and special way.

People who have read *I Will Lie Down In Peace* have written and told me how much the book 'spoke' to them. A young lady from Kerala, who had lost her husband a few years earlier, wrote, " I relived every moment of your struggle. I was never able to understand why it all happened the way it did or come to terms with it. Now I do understand. I feel as if you have written this book especially for me."

Many people say that reading this book has given them a different perspective on life. One young lady wrote, " I have been separated from my husband for a while, but after reading your book, I realized that your marriage is the kind of marriage I want for myself. So I am going back to join my husband to try again. Please pray for me."

During the days when Kumar was very sick and later after his death, the eternal WHY kept buzzing round in my head. Why us? Why so much needless suffering? My faith told me that everything works for good in the long run. I had to trust that somehow in God's grand plan, our suffering had a part. Maybe I would never know why during this lifetime. I wondered what good could possibly come out of all our suffering and pain. Two years later when I was plagued by these doubts again while writing this book, I received a letter from Bangalore: " I have given your book to my niece's family who are passing through the valley of darkness and need strength. Thank you for giving us this book. We needed it so badly."

The most poignant letter came from a young girl, " My father died when I was two, and I don't remember him at all. My mother never speaks to me about my father. After reading your book, I feel like I know my father. What he must have felt and the suffering he must have gone through. I am an only child and now I know how much my father must have loved me too. I know the kind of things he may have wanted to say to me. I feel as if you have written this book specially for me."

If someone had told me three years ago that people we didn't even know would one day be blessed by our suffering, I could not have accepted it. In fact I would have been very angry. But God moves in mysterious ways to perform His wonders and to bring people together. Had Kumar still been alive I would not have gone through these experiences and this book

A new life

would not have been written. Many people have been inspired by Kumar's story to find strength, meaning and renewal for their lives. Our gift of grief became special healing gifts for other people, and those who were healed in some way touched our lives too and made us feel very special.

When the children and I were on holiday in another city, we met a young lady who had read *I Will Lie Down In Peace*. She told me how much the book had meant to her and her family and enquired about how our lives had progressed since then. After we parted, I came to pay our hotel bill only to be told by the receptionist that my bill had already been paid. By the lady whom I had been talking to - "It was the least I could do, for what you gave us," she said, when I thanked her.

Almost every letter that came was a personal expression of affirmation and love. Letters came with prayers from people of different faiths from all over the world. So much love had disappeared almost overnight from our lives, but in a very special way, so much love was returned to us from people whom we could never have otherwise known or met.

The letters and calls keep coming. Some are desperately asking to see God's way and are groping for faith through terrible tragedies. Others just wanting someone to understand their pain, and listen to them. I think of David, whose wife committed suicide after a playful threat. Or Munuswamy who suffers from a painful disease that is gradually getting worse. Or Lata whose husband is dying of cancer; Jayan whose child has a heart problem. Susheela who lost her unborn child; Anandhi facing a painful divorce.

I have often wondered why this book has made an impact on people's lives and why people have responded so spontaneously to me as a writer. Maybe it is because most of us are unable to recognize the feelings that lie locked away in the deepest part of our hearts. We are unable to share our fears, our sadness, our confusions even with those closest to us, unable to find words to describe them; so when someone else does it for us, we feel a 'oneness' with that person. This discovery of 'oneness' makes us want to belong to someone whom we know understands how we feel and cares about us. This sense of belonging makes life precious and so different from that point on. In addition to this identification, the articulation of someone else's experience becomes the mirror in which another person can see more clearly what he or she has been experiencing only vaguely. It offers an opportunity to face situations and feelings he or she has been afraid of or unwilling to face. I feel blessed by the bond that I now share with so many people.

It seems strange that the loneliness and grief which once frightened and threatened to drown me, have now given me companionship and love which I could never have imagined earlier.

THE JOURNEY CONTINUES......

When death entered our family, it seemed as if life had stopped. When I started to pick up the threads of life again it was like going on a journey. A long journey where paths diverged in different directions. One path led through anger, self pity, frustrations and many negative feelings — another was a longer road – a harder road which required that I faced myself squarely and looked into my heart to understand my feelings, my desires and my goals honestly. It required constant emptying of negative feelings, of looking up towards God for healing and wholeness and coming to terms slowly with all that was lost. In acceptance and peace, not in anger and resignation.

I did not have to make the journey. I could quite easily have stayed where I was and still have survived. But it was important for me to move on and find new meaning to my life and for the children's. I needed to make this journey to discover a new identity for myself and to grow into the kind of woman I have always wanted to be....fearless, independent, creative and a healer.

Grief and loss are the most frightening, saddest experiences I have known so far. There was a time when I felt that I would never be healed of the pain and gloom that filled every part of my life. A time when I felt that I could not possibly earn a living to support myself and the children. When I felt that the intense loneliness that engulfed me would surely drown me.

In time, with the love and care from my family, my close friends and my faith in God, peace and strength slowly flowed into me. With it too came a brand new life and career. Grief which had once been frightening, now became a gift – a gift that I hadn't wanted, but was given anyway.

The children accepted their loss and grew up quickly in many ways. They became very protective of me and sensitive to my moods. They learnt to be aware of our finances in a new way and to be responsible about the house. They brought me flowers on my bad days and learnt to please me in little ways. The boys knew that I hated going out alone—they would give up a game of cricket, or a movie, or time with their friends to accompany me wherever I had to go and would jokingly brush aside my gratefulness by saying, "Can't afford to have you get lost somewhere Amma!" We learnt to knit our family together with a lot of love and humour.

One of the most important and lasting gifts that grief brought into my life is the loving and warm relationship I now share with my children. It has brought us to the point of trust and understanding — a relationship filled with laughter and humour even when things seem difficult. I have seen Jamie change from an easy going 'good time guy' to a more responsible young man with sound values and a purpose for his future. During this period John lost the vision in an eye due to an accident. There have been surgeries and it has been a time of pain, uncertainty and fear, not just for him, but for me as well. John too has changed from the shy, withdrawn, tense child into one who has accepted the limitations brought about by this accident. He still retains his great love for the outdoors and sports. The love and care between the brothers has also been strengthened in an unusual way. Mallika is only four years old and is blessed with musical and creative gifts. Already I see in her the soul of a healer, as she compassionately reaches out to anyone in pain. As a family we realized what our priorities are and what really matters in life. We learnt not to 'sweat the small stuff.'

Thus I began to look upon grief not as an enemy or an intruder into our lives but as a strange gift I received on my journey out of the labyrinth of pain. A gift that changed my attitudes, feelings and commitments to life. A gift that brought other people to me, and took me to those who needed me. A gift that transformed all my relationships. A gift that challenged me in every part of my life and helped me to grow in ways that I could otherwise not have imagined.

The period of grief was also a journey from a cold, barren, loveless place to one where it is warm and filled with surprises and joy and much love. Along the way many lessons were learnt. One of the most important being the awareness of how precious life is. How fragile. How wonderful. And how much we take it for granted. For a while after Kumar's death, we were aware of this and built our lives around this awareness. Each day was important for us. Every person we knew well was special. Each relationship, one to be treasured and enjoyed. But as the days went by, and as we got busier and into new routines, this awareness got left behind. Until we were rudely shaken by the sudden death of Kumar's younger brother just a year after he died.

"How fragile life is," I thought again. There were so many things we should have said to each other. There was so much to be resolved. Why didn't we do it when we had the chance? And now it was too late.

A few months later, another close friend died. There were regrets here too. A letter I should have written, a visit I should have made. Assurances I should have given. It seemed as if we had the best part of our lives ahead of us. Then suddenly it was gone – for ever.

I learnt that in life, we treasure that which is most fragile. When someone gives us a piece of hand—crafted crystal, we keep it in a special place where everyone can appreciate its beauty. We handle it with great care, lest it breaks. We have joy in knowing that it belongs to us. Its very fragility makes it most precious. In reality, that which is most fragile and most precious to us in life is not handcrafted crystal, but our relationships with each other. Yet, unlike crystal, we treat our relationships roughly. We abuse it with our selfishness. We discard it when we are tired of it. We betray it when something better comes along. We treat it like the least valuable thing in our life until something happens, and we lose it. Then we sadly realize how foolish we have been. It is this awareness of the fragility of life that enables me to nurture, enjoy and treasure

The journey continues......

all my relationships now and to put some of the difficult fractitious ones in order.

The loss of a loved one tears a family apart in many ways, and inlaws are often misunderstood at this time either for their excessive care, or their uncaring ways. For a long while my heart had been closed, angry and bitter. I realized that healing and moving forward with my life also depended on my reaching out to others in the family whom I had hurt, or who had hurt me. Asking forgiveness, with the hope of rebuilding a new relationship based on love and an understanding of each other, and the realization that life is indeed too fragile and precious to be wasted with pettiness, regrets and anger.

Knowing that my relationships are my most valuable assets which bring meaning, healing and joy to me has enabled me to rearrange my life to make more room than before for close friends, family and strangers. A local orphanage asked me to spend some time with their house mothers, talking to them and encouraging them in their daily lives. This kind of activity was way beyond my experience. I was reluctant to take it on mainly because it was time consuming and I had heard too that the women were difficult and sullen. During my first visit I encountered a handful of lonely, abandoned women, embittered by the blows life had dealt them. The monotonous routine of their lives, and the insular nature of community living had made them hard and unloving. No wonder they were difficult and sullen.

Each of us had a story to tell for we had been through different kinds of tragedies and had tried to rebuild our lives in different ways. For some the experience of rebuilding was successful, to others it brought no joy. For many, the loss of love from their lives had made them afraid to love again. Afraid of getting close to someone again. Afraid of being betrayed or rejected. So they protected themselves with a shield of hardness, coldness and harshness.

Beginning with myself, I initiated a sharing of experiences and feelings. The women followed, allowing themselves the luxury of delving into their depths and discovering the sources of their pain. Having discovered it, they had to face it again and live through the pain and finally allow it to leave their lives. The months spent with them opened up a new sense of awareness between us as women who had been broken in different ways. Our prayer was always the same,

Heal the hurt within us,
heal the memories that haunt us,
heal the feelings that drag us down.
Place within us the potential
to facilitate our own well-ness.
Be wholly in us,
who hunger for healing every day of our lives

As we shared our fears and revealed our deepest needs to each other, warmth, gentleness and humour flowed between us forging a bond of togetherness and a wonderful sense of belonging. We discovered that belonging to each other is a beautiful feeling. A joyous feeling of moving from loneliness to togetherness. In giving and receiving from each other we experienced the richness and fullness of life that is meant for us as human beings. We looked forward to our sessions together for it brought much healing of deep wounds, and opened us up to the wonderful power of love.

A passage from Henri Nouwen's *The Inner Voice Of Love*, written during the most difficult period of his life when he was recovering from the grief of loss meant a lot to me. The strength and comfort that this passage often gave me enabled me to move from anguish and despair, to hope, peace and an openness to love again. My experience of this passage and the insights learnt from it encouraged me to share it with them. Nouwen writes,

Do not hesitate to love, and to love deeply. When those you love deeply die, or leave you, or reject you, your heart will be broken. But that should not hold you back from loving deeply. The pain that comes from deep love…..is like a plough that breaks the ground to allow the seed to take root and grow into a strong plant. Every time you experience pain……you are faced with a choice. You can become bitter and decide not to love again, or you can stand straight in your pain and let the soil on which you stand become richer and more able to give life to new seeds.

Grief is a time which separates us from those who are not in grief. It makes us think of things that other people don't think of. It makes us feel things that others don't feel. It makes us more compassionate, more understanding, softer. It brings us closer to someone else's pain very quickly. The journey through grief has made me aware too of the brokenness in life all around - broken bodies, broken lives, broken dreams, broken hearts, broken minds, broken spirits, broken relationships.

The wife of a close friend who met with an accident

lay in a coma for months. The strain of the uncertainty and the hopelessness of the situation made him cry out in desperation for help one day. " I need someone to talk to. I need someone to share my pain with. I need someone to listen to me." There were several young people in our community who had been through suffering and loss of various kinds. We had a common bond. Although we all felt and understood his pain, we were unable to reach out to him or share our experiences with him or comfort him. We were too inhibited, too unsure of what he and others may think of us. Reaching out meant making ourselves vulnerable and open to pain all over again. It meant giving away a well preserved and locked up part of ourselves.

At this point I realized that the pain and wounds that each one of us carried from our own experiences is actually a channel of healing for someone else. It is only those who have passed through the valley of lonely suffering who can really reach out, sustain and comfort someone else. Thus getting together and sharing our experiences of pain, uncertainty and sadness was a precious gift we could give to our suffering friend.

So that is what we did. We met and shared our grief, our ways of coping, our faith, our explanations and insights into the mystery of pain and suffering with each other. We spoke about hope, faith and the final acceptance that sometimes brings healing and peace to our tortured souls. We shared too our persisting uncertainties and unanswered questions. We understood and upheld each person who had been through some kind of suffering. We cried and held each others's hands. We gave our confused and painful feelings words, and found that words are actually very important in healing...as they bring consolation, comfort and hope. They take away fear, isolation and guilt. They bring joy, understanding and peace. In sharing our personal grief we gave each other a very special gift that enriched us and brought tremendous peace and healing to all of us that evening.

We learnt that in a world full of broken people looking for answers, for hope, for some kind of meaning to their tragedies, those who have struggled with pain and suffering and have rebuilt their lives with faith, hope and love are like prophets and pointers to show others the way. The wounded person is in a better position to care for one whose wounds are still raw and bleeding. The wounded person in time becomes a healer. To be able to bind and soothe and heal has also been a gift that grief has given me.

Healing, I discovered, is never a straight line. It is a case of one step forward, two steps back. There are many set backs. Sometimes little things build up—tiredness, a cold remark, someone else's thouhghlessness, a memory thought to be buried that pops up unexpectedly—it feels as if you have been pulled off the road, and the little ground gained feels lost. There are still days when everything is grey and dismal...when I weep...when the loneliness drives me crazy. Sometimes it feels as if there is a turbulent river of anguish just below the surface. Wave after wave ebbs and flows. On such gloomy days I make sure that a vase of beautiful flowers is on the table. I cook an extra special meal for the family and invite someone who is lonelier than me. Then the grey day becomes a festive one—with company and laughter and love.

Often I feel that I need a close relationship with another person to be able to live normally. To be a 'whole' person. To be lovable. To be able to love. To live well and meaningfully, to have a sense of well being. I long to wake up to the day when there will be no twinge of sadness or loneliness or tears. Once after a long period of calm when I thought I was over the worst, a hymn sung at church caused me to break down and weep Angry with myself for losing my peace I cried out to a friend, "Why am I still crying after all this time. Why does it still hurt so much?" He revealed that almost sixteen years after the death of his child, a sudden memory of her caused him to weep in public. " There will always be a wound when there is love, and it is lost. You need not apologize for your tears. It is the most natural thing to happen." His sharing gave me the strength to cope with my somewhat wayward emotions.

Much later, I met a lady who had lost her teenage son several years earlier. As she related the incident, tears flowed from her eyes. " I'm so sorry, I shouldn't be crying after all this time," she said helplessly. I remembered my friend's experience and his words to me and gave them to her. Holding each other's hands, our tears freely flowing, bringing healing to each other, we understood that there will always be a wound when love is lost. Being a wounded healer is a gift that goes on and on. It gets passed from one person to another.

Every grieving person is like a bruised reed, vulnerable, and weak, with numerous roots that no one else can see. The storms that blow from time to time have the power to uproot trees, and devastate life. The ordinary reed when battered by wild winds may bend and

The journey continues...... 89

sway and flatten out for a while. But in time it will straighten out slowly. That is the way God intended it to be. So too with each person burdened by pain and grief and loss.

> *God's ability to restore life is beyond our understanding.*
> *Forests burn, and grow back.*
> *Broken bones heal,*
> *Grief turns into joy.*
> *God brings good out of tragedy.*

The sense of loss will remain, but there is a Divine love which if we are open to it, will reach out to us in many unexpected ways. It may not come to us in the way that we have been looking for, or in the way that we want. But in unexpected and surprising ways God's love will reach out to us and heal.

I can see now that grief—which once was an impossible burden—has in time become a source of endless gifts for me which I discovered on my journey from anguish and pain to peace and hope. What once seemed like a terrible curse, has actually turned out to be a blessing.

During this journey I learnt too that joy does not simply happen to us. It does not come to us on a plate, wrapped with a red bow. It is something that we have to consciously choose over sorrow. The act of deliberately choosing joy is the greatest challenge and requires much energy. It is so much easier to slink into the swamps of self pity and sorrow. For a while it was painful looking at photographs of us as a whole family. We had studiously avoided taking a new family photograph. A friend from overseas sent us two beautifully framed pictures – one of us with Kumar, and one of just the children and me. As I placed them side by side on my desk I realized that I had a choice......either to look at them and remember the loss....and focus on the missing person . .....or to be joyous that we all looked so good and happy in both pictures. It is in making this choice, that I allowed myself to heal.

On my desk beside the photograph I placed a poem by the poet Khalil Gibran,

Your joy is your sorrow unmasked.......
When you are joyous, look deep into your heart and you shall find
it is only that which has given you sorrow that is giving you joy.
When you are sorrowful look again in your heart, and you shall see
that in truth you are weeping for that which has been your delight.

I discovered that grief is more than just the loss brought by death, and that for some, it is a never ending nightmare and a constant source of pain. This knowledge has enabled me to open my arms, my heart and my home to offer hospitality not just to my friends but also to strangers in need of comfort and healing. The dining table, I discovered is a place for great intimacy and healing. At the end of a meal a young friend who had a wonderful career, a beautiful home and an exciting lifestyle broke down over the agony of not being able to have a child. Everybody thought she was a career girl and had opted out not to have a family. The anguish which for many years had been well hidden under a carefully cultivated manner suddenly surfaced and she was able to share her pain and talk it over with someone. Many times around our table over a simple meal I have been given the opportunity to affirm, encourage, and comfort someone.

The long journey through grief taught me to knock off my pride in my independence and in my abilities and to forget that 'I don't need anyone. I can do it by myself.' It taught me the humility of reaching out for help and the joy of receiving it. It also brought me closer to my brothers and their families as they helped me rebuild my life. Although I was not very close to the extended family of my in-laws, our shared grief, and their concern for us which manifested itself through letters, visits and gifts for me and the children, helped to bind us closer together.

I learnt too the value of simplicity and cleared my life of all useless clutter. At the beginning of a journey we travel with all our baggage. What if it rains? We need something for that. What if we fall ill…..surely we need something for that too? What if we get bored? So too we carry the unnecessary unwanted baggage of our emotions and feelings. But as we journey further we come to a point where we are surer of ourselves, where we know what we really need, and throw away all the useless baggage that just weighs us down.

Through the long journey I experienced the richness, the warmth of love and friendship that so many people brought into our lives at every stage. I discovered that the closer we become to one another, the more we allow another person to become a part of us, the more 'alive' and 'human' we are. The more connected we are to another person, the more meaning there is in our lives.

And finally, the journey brought me closer to God. My relationship with God became more personal, more intense, more trusting, more alive. Knowing that there is never a time when I am far from . His presence, knowing that He provides for my every need, knowing that He is the companion of my soul at all times. This has enabled me to accept grief as a special and wonderful gift.

The years that lie behind , with all the struggles and anguish will perhaps be remembered finally as the path that led from the cold bleak winter of life, to where I stand today......in the freshness of spring, with new life and new visions. It is good to know that when winter comes......spring is not far behind.

Copyright Acknowledgments

From EMBRACING GOD'S WORLD by Joyce Hugget
Copyright @1996 by Joyce Hugget, Hodder and Stoughton

From THE INNER VOICE OF LOVE
By Henri J. M. Nouwen
Copyright @ 1996 and 1997 Henri J. M. Nouwen, Darton, Longman and Todd.

From A GRIEF OBSERVED By C.S. Lewis
Copyright @ 1961 C.S.Lewis, Faber and Faber

From YOU SURPRISED ME By Joe Mannath
Copyright @1987 by Joe Mannath,SDB,
Chair Publications

From THE PROPHET By Khalil Gibran
THE HOLY BIBLE,

AND IF I GO by Collen Cora Hitchcock

IF I COULD BEAR THE BURDEN by Renee Duval